What Writers Do

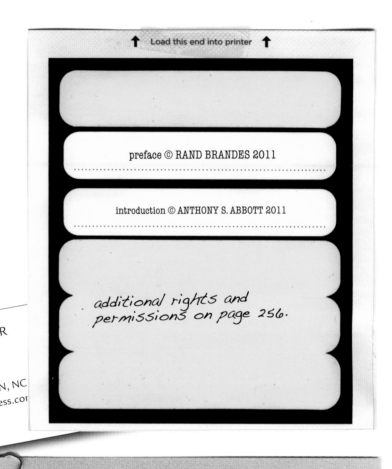

Load this end into printer

preface © RAND BRANDES 2011

introduction © ANTHONY S. ABBOTT 2011

additional rights and
permissions on page 256.

PUBLISHER

DAVIDSON, NC
lorimerpress.com

LORIMER
PRESS

"What Writers Do" is funded in part by a Project Pool's grant from the United Arts Council of Catawba County.

ISBN: 978-0-9826171-7-5
Library of Congress Control Number: 2011930681

book designer: Leslie Rindoks

Printed in China

What Writers Do

a celebration of
Lenoir-Rhyne University's
Visiting Writers Series

series editor
Rand Brandes

volume editor
Anthony S. Abbott

Abigail DeWitt's writing space

PREFACE

What Writers Do is the first in a series of publications dedicated to document-
ing over twenty years of outstanding literary programming presented by
Lenoir-Rhyne University's Visiting Writers Series. Since its inception in 1988,
the Series has hosted almost two hundred regionally, nationally and interna-
tionally recognized authors. These authors and their works represent an
array of literary genres that reflect the diversity of our campus and commu-
nities. *What Writers Do* is comprised of a cross-section of writers who have
read as part of the Series over the years. As the seasonal metaphor that
shapes the book suggests, the list of writers grew organically beginning at the
center with writers from our earliest years and extending to the outer rings
of our most recent.

What Writers Do includes work by a Nobel Laureate, US Poet Laureate, North
Carolina State Laureates, and a wide range of literary award and prize-win-
ners. Many of the writers participated in the Series long before their
audiences grew and their writing was "officially" recognized to be of the
highest caliber. In addition, a few of these writers like Billy Collins, Ron Rash,
Kathryn Stripling Byer and Tony Abbott, were also Visiting Writers-in-
Residence at Lenoir-Rhyne and have provided invaluable classroom
instruction for our students. All of the authors have captured our imagina-
tions and shaped the searcher in all of us.

What Writers Do embodies not only the Writers Series' commitment to high-
quality and diversified writing, but also the spirit of the program and its
mission "to build a community of readers." Since reading is such a solitary
experience, bringing readers together provides an opportunity to share our
passion for the written word and to open ourselves up to the transformative
potential of the spoken word. The stories, poems, essays, and interviews in
What Writers Do reflect the energy of our events where we are entertained,
educated, and enlightened. Each season was unique as a result of changing
campus initiatives, community partnerships, and themes.

Thanks to on-going support from Lenoir-Rhyne University, individual patrons, local corporations and organizations, and our local and state Arts Councils, all Visiting Writers Series events are free and open to the public. A recent gift of 1.7 million dollars from a friend of the Series will help guarantee that they will remain so and that the community will always feel welcome. *What Writers Do* will make it possible for audiences to hear their favorite Writers Series authors in their homes and to share our wonderful evenings with their friends.

What Writers Do represents the collaborative nature of the best literary publishing endeavours. As volume editor and contributor, Tony Abbott continues his life-long commitment to fostering creative writing and writers in North Carolina. Leslie Rindoks at Lorimer Press put her many talents into making this a finely designed and distinctive book, pleasing to the inner and outer eye. Lisa Hart, Special Projects Coordinator for the Visiting Writers Series kept the lines of communication open and deadlines met. Finally, I want to thank our contributors for helping to establish the growing reputation of the Series and for returning to campus in the spirit of their works.

Rand Brandes
Series Editor
Director, Lenoir-Rhyne University Visiting Writers Series

* And a note of gratitude to all our contributors for providing a deeper look into what it is writers do. (And for satisfying our voyeuristic tendencies by showing us *where the magic happens!*) To Abigail DeWitt and Robert Inman, special thanks for also providing early drafts of their work.

Dedicated to the Visiting Writers Series'
Steering Committee Members
– present and past –
and to our outstanding
Student Assistants through the years.

TABLE OF CONTENTS

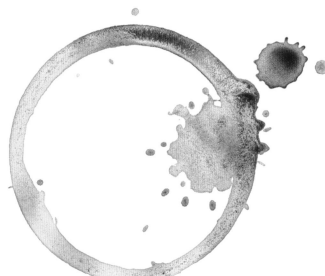

It began with an idea: literature is life-changing. The writing of a story or a poem may be life-changing for the writer, the reading of that story or poem or essay might be life-changing for the reader. The experience depicted in the literary work might be life-changing for the central character. I liked that idea, and when we wrote letters to the writers who had participated in the Lenoir-Rhyne University Visiting Writers Series, we asked them to send us something life-changing. Here is the result—thirty-seven pieces by thirty-three different writers: nineteen poems, eleven essays, seven stories, and an interview. These pieces are divided into four sections, and each section has its own themes, its own flavor and character. Each section is virtually a season.

In the first section, we ask: What do writers do? And it is no accident that the book begins with Joseph Bathanti's haunting essay, "Ghost, Come Back Again," the story, both poignant and funny, of his birth as a writer on his visit to the Thomas Wolfe House in Asheville when he was just twenty-three years old. As a result of his visit, he immerses himself wholly in Wolfe and begins his first novel, his very own *Look Homeward, Angel*. One thing writers do is read. Anna Quindlen tells us "How Reading Changed My Life" and celebrates the very touch and feel of books. Julia Alvarez survives the month of March in Vermont by writing a haiku a day to keep the doctor away. Josephine Humphreys gets on a train at seventeen and meets a beautiful Lumbee girl on her way to meet her young husband's parents. She is afraid the parents will hate her because she is not white. Humphreys' life was completely changed by this encounter, which led her years later to write her powerful novel about the Lumbee, *Nowhere Else on Earth*. What do writers do? They create art, and art keeps us young. In Donald Secreast's fascinating story, "Whose Woods These Are," the central character, Peyton Gilley, stays young forever by crafting chairs out of wood. The wood quite literally becomes his life.

1

Joe Pike in Robert Inman's *Dairy Queen Days* crafts a motorcycle and then must live the life he imagines as an artist. His art keeps him alive. Joan McBreen's beautiful poem, "February Song" celebrates the beauty and longing of "the woman who writes at a table." In this section of the collection, we see that art itself is enough, or almost enough.

In Part Two we feel a profound dislocation. In Part One the writer is the central figure. Art itself is redemptive. In this section we are in the world, and the redemption of the world is hard. It is not the artist who can redeem the world, but someone in and of the world, or perhaps someone who transcends the world like the extraordinary Jesus of Reynolds Price's vision in *A Whole New Life.*

The world is dark. The woman at the pond in Ron Rash's story has been beaten by her boyfriend. The women in Sharon Olds' extraordinary poem, "Reading the Paper," have been denied the right to read or write. Jordan in *Theatrics* is very nearly overwhelmed by the reality of her world controlled by the drugs which she uses and the men who use her. The stained glass windows of the church in Nathalie Anderson's poem, "De Profundis" seem to depict only images of war and slaughter. In *The Power of Love,* the black people of South Africa suffer brutally under the long, tyrannical rule of apartheid. Robert Hedin depicts the power of a tornado, and Reynolds Price describes the excruciating pain from the spinal tumor he calls "the eel."

If it is partly the function of the writer to depict such a world truthfully, honestly, it is also the writer's task to answer the question—what can be done? Sometimes the answer seems to be—nothing. In Mark Powell's piece and in Ron Rash's there are no solutions. But in Rhett Trull's poems the darkness is alleviated by another person, a person who walks into the darkness of the narrator's life at just the right moment. Robert Hedin's poem, "The Greatest" celebrates the presence of Mohammed Ali in the life of a suffering Kurdish boy in northern Iraq. In *The Power of Love* the wisdom and charisma of Nelson Mandela combat the darkness of apartheid with the power of love, and in Reynolds Price it is the mysterious Jesus who promises to eventually heal the writer's body and soul. But the healing, in this section of the book, is never complete, only hoped for and promised.

In the third part, the healing is fully present. I like to think of this section as almost a continuous celebration of life. Death is present in Jill McCorkle's splendid story which opens the section, but this is not a story about death, it is a celebration of the father's life, the life which he has passed on to his daughter, who gives it back to him when he dies with the absolute beauty and clarity of her words. We can almost say that the theme of this section is language—the power of language to heal and to celebrate. We have Billy Collins' marvelous poem, "Irish Poetry" that makes us feel tangibly the force of the Irish tongue, and the Irishman himself, Frank McCourt, who is able, by the sheer power of his language, to convert his high school classroom into a place of joy and glee despite the disapproval of the chagrined administration. Cathy Smith Bowers celebrates her dog, Seamus, lost in her divorce, whose picture she carries in her wallet, whose "bark" becomes the very title of the poem. John Updike, that master user of language, talks about his stammer in astonishingly eloquent terms. Richard Chess speaks of how the "Mystery of Parents" in their love for their children can redeem ordinary time, and Kay Byer redeems the ordinary through her lovely evocation of the fragility of the end of autumn in "Awake." Abigail DeWitt takes us inside the heart and soul of a teen-age girl experiencing love for the first time just before an allied bomb falls on her house in the story ironically titled, "Liberation." She and the boy find their liberation in words, words that change her from a girl into a woman.

In Part Four, we have made the cycle of a year. The book opens with snow falling in Boone, NC in Joseph Bathanti's essay. It ends with Fred Chappell's marvelous poem, "Flakes," which allows us to experience through his language the miracle of snow. ". . .the snow finds that everything that was lost is not lost," he reminds us. In fact, maybe the theme of this section is miracle, or if not miracle, then love. Maybe the theme is best stated in Sharon Olds' powerful poem, "What Thou Lovest Well." "…what thou lovest well remains, the rest is dross" she quotes Ezra Pound as saying. And nowhere in this whole collection is that saying more fully embodied than in Lee Smith's astonishing memoir to her son, Josh, in "Goodbye to the Sunset Man." The essay is one of the purest acts of love I have ever encountered in literature, and when I set out to edit this anthology, I asked Lee for that piece, because it changed my life. So many of the pieces in this final section are celebrations of either miracles or love or both. The miracle in Eleanor Tate's "What Goes Around Comes Around" turns out to be a very wise and loving grandmother. It is the love of the "you" in Nikki Giovanni's stunning poem "Inventory" that keeps the narrator from despair. It is the wisdom and courage of Mitchell Gold that saves dozens of gay young people from doing active harm to themselves. Sam Gwynn remembers all his favorite poems with astounding virtuosity as he approaches a significant birthday. Brett Lott receives a letter from a former student that totally changes his life as a writing teacher. And then there is Fred Chappell's snow which ends the book.

So maybe I got what I asked for, poems, stories, essays that change people's lives. In an age when so much we read is either dreary or unintelligible, it is a joy to find a group of writers who can celebrate life and language and hope. They give us courage. They make us want to be the human beings we were intended to be. They make us want to use the language in new and better ways and to honor the dignity and power of the old ways. At the end of "God's Grandeur," Hopkins writes, "There lives the dearest freshness deep down things." These writers have discovered that freshness and they have passed it on to us as a gift. Now we must unwrap the present.

—*Anthony S. Abbott*

PART ONE

GHOST, COME BACK AGAIN
Joseph Bathanti

It had started to snow on our tiny yellow cottage in Shuffletown as dusk came on and, when the call came from Patricia, there were probably six inches in our backyard – a rarity in that part of the North Carolina Piedmont. I sat on the living room's garish calico shag carpet, leaning against the baseboard heater. Phoebe Snow's *It Looks Like Snow* played on our Goodwill turntable. Joan and I had opened a bottle of red wine; we figured we were in for the night.

Patricia wanted Joan and me to drive to Boone. It was snowing like mad up there and she and her boyfriend Dave were having a party at her house on Poplar Creek Road. They had been our great friends on Oakland Avenue in Charlotte where we'd lived just before and after marrying, and we hadn't seen them since we'd all split for different precincts. Through the phone, I heard jubilation in the background. I told Patricia that we were besieged by snow ourselves and settled in. We were going to sit tight. Joan was fine with that. It made no sense to get on the road. It was nine o'clock. We were alone, happy, drinking wine in the middle of a white-out in Shuffletown.

The phone rang again. This time it was Dave. He made the same plea as Patricia, but more passionately with that inflection of challenge. Again, I heard those Appalachian State kids raising hell in the background. They were having a good time. *Where was I?* He made me feel like I was missing something. It was December of 1979. I was 26. Joan had just turned 24.

We grabbed a few things and jumped into our VW Squareback and headed north on Highway 16. I didn't consult a map. Maybe I got directions from Dave. It was snowing so hard we couldn't make out the bridge as we crossed the Catawba into Gaston County, just a mile into our journey. Mountain Island Lake stretched silver toward the chuffing stacks of the mysterious power plant on the water. Laura's Rozzelle House, last of the mythic Southern all-you-can-eat family-style manses, kept its counsel on the near bank, and Thomas Wolfe, as he often did, chanted in my head: *O lost, and by the wind grieved, ghost come back again.*

I visited the North Carolina mountains for the first time before we married. Joan and I, then living in Charlotte, travelled west on Independence Boulevard until it became a dizzying two lane switchback. By the time we fetched Asheville, we were sick with vertigo, and the city seemed nothing like Scott and Zelda's Shangri la. Downtown Asheville, in 1976 was dank and haggard. Like one the little steel towns that dotted the banks of the three big rivers that swept out of my hometown Pittsburgh. I liked Asheville very much. We had reached a pinnacle. Joan and I walked among clouds that sailed like dirigibles across the sky, their shadows falling across the face of the bluish mountains. I had never stood at such altitude.

I had only heard of Thomas Wolfe. I owned a copy of *You Can't Go Home Again* (if nothing else, its title seemed apropos of a cruel inevitability), a Signet paperback that sold new for 95 cents, ten years before in 1966, though the great big novel first appeared in 1940. I had figured to one day read it, but never had. In fact, I managed to earn a Master's Degree in English Literature from the University of Pittsburgh without ever reading a word by Thomas Wolfe. In all likelihood, back then, I conflated Thomas Wolfe with Tom Wolfe, the white linen-suited new journalist, who wrote *The Electric Kool-Aid Acid Test.*

That weekend, as Joan and I strolled Asheville, we came upon Old Kentucky Home (called Dixieland in Wolfe's first novel, *Look Homeward, Angel*), Thomas Wolfe's boyhood home, a 29 room Queen Anne boarding house, painted white, built in 1883 – turrets and gables and porches mitered into the upper stories – ramrodded by his imperious mother, Julia Wolfe. It had been kept over the years as a literary shrine to the memory of Wolfe. Joan swooned indiscriminately over all things educational – she was trained as a teacher at the University of Georgia – the more antique the better. Touring someone's home did not interest me. But I would have done anything to please her, not to mention that I wished to come off as urbane. Plus, I wanted to be a writer – had indeed begun composing my first stories in our cramped attic garret in Charlotte we lived in at the time – and I was well aware that Wolfe had been a famous one. Something must have happened in those sprawling plaster rooms he had begun living in at age 6, before departing in 1916 to matriculate at the state university in Chapel Hill.

We paid to get in, then ambled the museum-like rooms, decked in the period livery and accoutrement of Wolfe's era. The house had the funereal, mausoleum aura of the Pompei ruins – as if the family had moments before been spirited away, but left everything in pristine shape for expected company – half a century later. The rooms I entered had no real significance for me. Again, I hadn't read a solitary syllable Wolfe had penned. Joan enjoyed the house for its curios and furniture, its palpable witness of the vanished *noblesse oblige* of mythic Southern lore. She hailed from *Gone with the Wind* country, Atlanta, and she wore back then, when I first met her, a mantle of fierce love of everything south of the Mason-Dixon, the further south the better. I heard her once say that North Carolina was getting a little too far north. She was still in her Yankee-loathing phase, and her abiding suspicion of them was unrelenting. Somehow I had earned clemency. I was a Yankee, she'd grudgingly admit, but not a damn Yankee.

As I wandered the rooms, I had no idea that I was laying eyes on W.O. Wolfe's actual stone cutter's tools, that the grand fireplace I glanced at was where W.O. and then his counterpart from *Look Homeward, Angel*, Oliver Gant, doused the laid hearth in kerosene of a morning and with a single match set off a blaze like a rocket to warm his children. Nor the very china and flatware, the tureens, and pitchers Julia Wolfe and then her fictional doppelganger, Eliza Gant, set before her strange boarders. The room, the very bed, where Benjamin Harrison Wolfe, Thomas's brother would die in and then die in again, still Ben, his name not changed in the fiction, *In Look Homeward, Angel*. It was all there, spread before me; I just didn't know what it was.

Then I crossed the threshold of a bedroom, upstairs, and in an opened closet hung a massive camel-hair topcoat, swaying almost imperceptibly in whatever breath suspired throughout that house. Beneath it on the floor sat a pair of enormous plain brown oxfords, the laces untied as if Wolfe had just stepped out of them. On a table in the middle of the room brooded a solemn black typewriter – an antique Remington or Olivetti, the name flourished in gold above the tiered keyboard. Light sluiced through the white sheer curtains. The very last of it burnishing that coat and shoes, flashing off the gilt keys of the typewriter.

It was the end of the day – beatified with all the ineffability with which Wolfe wrote. I stood in that room with the woman I loved – she really believed that some day I'd be a writer – and something occurred that my Catholic disposition, even now, latches onto as the gift of grace. I found myself miraculously transformed into a Thomas Wolfe fanatic, evangelized, I swear, by his topcoat and shoes. Nothing more poignant, nor memorable. And most astonishing of all, I had never read a word he'd written.

That deficit, however, was quickly remedied. I like to think I rushed out of Old Kentucky Home, aglow like Paul after he was knocked off his horse on the road to Damascus, to the nearest bookstore and purchased everything authored by Wolfe they carried. I had found my author. What I do know is that I launched into a pathological and exhaustive study of Thomas Wolfe. Appropriately, I launched first into *Look Homeward, Angel* and was "touched by that dark miracle of chance which makes new magic in a dusty world." I adored the book. Then onto *Of Time and the River*, and the Wolfe biography by Elizabeth Nowell, Wolfe's literary agent; and *The Letters of Thomas Wolfe,* edited by Nowell. I ripped through *The Window of Memory,* by Richard Kennedy; *The Mountains,* edited by Pat Ryan, a book containing Wolfe's plays; the biographies *Aline* by Carole Klein, about Wolfe's lover, Aline Bernstein; and A. Scott Berg's wonderful *Max Perkins: Editor of Genius.* I read *Thomas Wolfe and His Family,* by Mable Wolfe Wheaton (Wolfe's sister, portrayed as Helen in *Look Homeward, Angel*), with LeGette Blythe. I even tackled *Thomas Wolfe: The Critical Reception,* edited by Paschal Reeves, a compendium of reviews, scholarly abstracts and précis – the kinds of writing that in my former life I had carefully steered clear of because of how tawdry and boring I found them. Joan and I visited Wolfe's grave at Riverside Cemetery. I had more or less lost my mind.

By the time we moved out of Charlotte to Shuffletown, I had pusselgutted myself on Thomas Wolfe. There, in the yellow cottage, I had a little room off our living room and, at a wooden table I had nailed together myself, I began my first novel, an unapologetically swooning bildungsroman in homage to Wolfe that I called, in the overwrought spirit of Wolfe, *Perhaps, by Love Bequeathed.* It was, of course, about growing up in Pittsburgh, the city lately called the Paris of Appalachia – a stretch for anyone who's ever visited that not obviously Appalachian city – though perhaps some muse of my homeland's geography, its hills, coal barges and steel, its hardheaded devotion to grime and toil and hardscrabble had infiltrated my consciousness, my soul, as I set out to mimic Thomas Wolfe. He had wanted to say everything: in a never before apprehended mad poetic epistemological rant, sheer unbridled passion, the more the better – and so did I, not unlike I'm certain other unwashed writers just starting out.

I worked on my book every day in joy and certainty – some of the most inspired and glorious writing I've ever bent my head over and I'll always be grateful for those days sitting there basking in the unlikely and utter dazzle that I was a genius, the heir apparent to Wolfe. Were I attached to cigarettes, I would have chain-smoked. Had I been able, I would have stood and used the top of our refrigerator to write on – as Wolfe had done – but I wasn't tall enough. Instead I sat and wrote everything out long-hand in tiny immaculate cursive on a legal pad, then typed the day's yield on my old Underwood, using carbon paper to produce a second copy. I was writing my own family saga, filled with melodrama and tenderness and oozing with heartbreaking flowery sentimentality, channeling the gargantuan Wolfe – and he never let me down. I let it all go in that over-the-top frenzy of words he was so famous for: three-four adjectives for every noun. Pages filled in a weir of impenetrable, impressionistic language that I told myself made sense. Words and more words – that I counted over and over. Output was everything. Somewhere I had read that Wolfe, after a feast at Cherio's, his favorite restaurant, lumbered through Manhattan on one of his legendary interminable treks muttering a litany of "I wrote ten thousand words today, I wrote ten thousand words today."

Like Wolfe, I drank indecent amounts of coffee as I wrote. Cup after cup, pot after pot, until I was so deranged with caffeine I'd barge out our front door and yawp barbarically at the crows in the pine trees ringing the cottage and they'd yawp back in affirmation. I refused food until nightfall, then fell asleep dreaming about what I'd written that day, what I'd write the next. I was certain that what I scribed at that table in Shuffletown was good, damn good, that it would guarantee my fame as a writer, that when I sat in that room I was in the grip of something wholly original. The Muse had its claws lodged in my capacious heart. There's a good chance I was never happier.

That night we left Shuffletown for my second trip to the North Carolina mountains, this time to Boone, in Watauga County, I was very much under the spell of Thomas Wolfe. It was experience I was after and the caprice that night in the blizzard proved worth it. Joan and I would only realize a day later on our return, when we could actually see the skinny winding roads hanging over the escarpments we'd travelled to get there, how insane we'd been to attempt the journey in the first place.

Somehow we made it up the mountain. I remember inching up Poplar Creek Road, on the fringe of Appalachian's campus, peering into the driving snow for our friend's house when at us came a brigade of wild kids on skis tooling down the middle of the road to welcome us, the heroic wayfarers we fancied ourselves. Later that night, after much good cheer and revelry, and the onset of desperate hunger, the most miraculous event of the evening occurred. Patricia picked up the phone for take-out – Joan and I gasped in incredulity – and in short order a Jeep commandeered by an intrepid grinning kid grinded up with a sack of meatball sandwiches from Sollecito's, an Italian joint that delivered in blizzards at 3 a.m. *Holy God*, I thought, standing in the middle of the road in a foot and a half of snow eating the indescribably delicious sandwich, *I want to live here.* I never dreamed that, twenty-two years later, I would land a job teaching creative writing at Appalachian State University, that those inscrutable amazing mountains that shrouded my future that snowy night long ago would become my beloved home.

Of course, my Thomas Wolfe novel was no good, but it took a little while before that fact hit me. I don't apologize for it not being good. It's no secret that one has to write poorly before writing well. Nevertheless, that realization came with true regret and reluctantly I scrapped my book. Not long after, I lost traction with Wolfe as well and never made it all the way through *The Web and the Rock*, and I still haven't read *You Can't Go Home Again* – though I'll always love Wolfe and will be forever grateful to him, to his overcoat and shoes, to whatever happened to me the day I traipsed into Old Kentucky Home. I'm willing to call it mystical. It made me want to write a book every day, to fill my own steamer trunk with stained and tattered foolscap.

FEBRUARY SONG

Joan McBreen

Lift the latch, enter the room,
stand in silence behind the woman
who writes at a table, facing a window.
She learns what lines and shadows teach
while rain threatens the fading light.
She knows that you left a cafe
to buy her anemones,
that the world's promises
given and stolen
are not the enemy,
that you will be there
when she turns towards you.

CARDIFF, MARCH 1995
Joan McBreen

Suddenly, the afternoon turned cold,
the city seemed to still, the sky
darkened. Rain began to fall.

The peaches in her bag were ripe.
She had bought them cheap.
Nonetheless they would taste good.

He came towards her along the street,
holding mock orange blossom
wrapped in white paper.

She took them from him.
In her right hand were the peaches,
in the other she held the flowers.

She could not wipe the rain
or tears from her face.

21-7-2010

HOW READING CHANGED MY LIFE
Anna Quindlen

I wrote fiction in college, and then for many years I wrote fact, as best I could gather, discern, and describe it, as a newspaper reporter. Then I wrote fiction again. Reading taught me how to do it all.

"Books are over," the editor of a journal to be found only on the Internet told me one day at a conference on the future of the newspaper business. Just my luck. After all these years of reading books I'd finally written one; when I took time to alphabetize my shelves, it came between Proust and Ayn Rand, which seemed representative of how I'd read all my life, between the great and the merely engagingly popular. I could still remember the time I had held my first hardcover book. The Federal Express truck raised a cloud of gravel and dust on a country road as I ripped into the envelope, removed the book, and lifted it up and down in my outstretched hands, just to feel the heft of it, as though it was to be valued by weight. I held it the way I'd seen babies held at religious ceremonies, a bris, perhaps, or a baptism. Hardcovers: every writer's ultimate ambition, whether she admits it or not.

It was a fearsome frisson that ripped through the business, the business of writing, the business of publishing, the business of newspapering, when I was well into all three. The computer had become like the most miraculous sort of technological Swiss Army knife: each time you thought you knew what it could do, it turned out that it could do more, faster, better, more accurately. I wrote my first novel on a big clunker of a machine that wheezed slightly when it stored information and had a mere 256 kilobits of memory. It just managed to hold the book, the word-processing program, and a few other odds and ends. My third novel was composed on a machine that fits into my handbag and weighs slightly more than a premature baby.

The program corrects my punctuation and capitalization as I type; when I try to type a stand-alone lowercase I, it inflates it into a capital letter, correcting me peremptorily, certain I've made a mistake. 1 could keep a dozen copies of my book on its hard disk and it wouldn't even breathe hard.

And there was less than a decade between the publication of those two books.

So it became easy, as the age of the computer washed in a wave of modems and cybersurfers over the United States at the end of the twentieth century, to believe those who said that books need never leave the soul of this new machine at all, that the wave of the future was this: *The Age of Innocence* on-line, to be called up and read with the push of a view button; *The Fountainhead* via the Internet, perhaps with all the tiresome objectivist polemical speeches set in a different font for easy skipping-over (or even the outright deletions that Ayn Rand's editor should have taken care of). No paper, no shelf space, and the ultimate democratization of reading: a library in a box much smaller than a single volume of the old leatherbound *Encyclopedia Britannica*. To all the old fears–of lack of literacy, of interest, of quality–was added the fear of microchips.

A small skirmish in these technowars broke out in the summer of 1997 in the pages of *The Horn Book*, the journal of children's literature, and it was representative of both the worst-case scenarios and the realities of the future of publishing in an era of tearaway technology. A writer and librarian named Sarah Ellis tried an experiment: she read on a laptop computer a book for children called *The End of the Rainbow*. But this was not just any book: it exemplified the greatest fears of those who love children's literature, and know how difficult it can be to publish in a cost-conscious age. *The End of the Rainbow* was part of a series of Danish books about a boy named Buster published by Dutton; the sales trajectory of its predecessors had convinced the publisher to offer it free on the Internet rather than go to the expense of publishing it in book form.

Ms. Ellis gave Buster on the computer a fair shake, but she found the experience ultimately unsatisfactory. She concluded that the process of scrolling down, reading in a linear fashion, on a machine she associates with haste, were all antithetical to reading for pleasure. "The screen," she says, "turned me into a reluctant reader." When she went to the library and took out an earlier bound Buster book, her reluctance disappeared. "I experienced that feeling of surrender, of putting myself in someone's hands, which is one of the great pleasures of fiction," she wrote. And she reclaimed the experience of a book, pure and simple: "the soft scrape of my fingers against the pages, the glissando sound of flipping back to a previous chapter." The scrolling of the screen had not been the equivalent of turning the pages. A laptop is portable, but not companionable.

Ms. Ellis believed her experiment raised many questions about the future of reading in the face of the ascendancy of computers, questions that will be raised over and over again in the years to come. But, reading her words, I found more questions answered than asked, and one essential one settled to my satisfaction. At the time that technocrats had predicted the imminent death of the book as we knew it, all of us in the world of print were in a kind of a frenzy about how new technology would change our old businesses. In the five years between my first job as a copy girl and my hiring at *The New York Times* as a reporter, big papers had begun to retire their typewriters and bring in computer systems on which reporters would produce the day's copy and editors edit it. It was a modest revolution, given the advances still to come, but a revolution not without pain, one of the *Times*'s most venerable reporters insisted he was too old to learn new tricks, and his copy had to be transcribed into the computer from the copy paper he continued to use in his old manual typewriter.

But the real revolution was said to be coming in the product itself. Panel after panel was held at journalism conventions about whether newspapers would be replaced by the downloading of the day's news onto a computer screen. It seemed only sensible to those whose correspondence had become characters sent by modem from one computer to another instead of a file of business letters, inevitable that the collection of folded newsprint that landed on the doormat with a *thwap* before daybreak each morning could simply be replaced by a virtual newspaper in a computer in the kitchen, coffee cup beside the keyboard.

Perhaps that may someday come to pass, in one form or another; perhaps someday it will seem quaint that anyone ever doubted that the printed book between hard or soft covers was in its twilight at the end of the twentieth century. But the decade after the initial panic over the demise of printing upon paper seemed to foreshadow a very different end. News indeed appeared on computers; so did magazines, some created expressly for online users. There were even books like the Buster book that Dutton put on the Internet rather than risk commercial failure. But none of them convincingly supplanted the more conventional product. Both those in the business of books and those in the business of computer technology realized something that we readers apprehended most deeply in our hearts: that people are attached, not only to what is inside books, but to the object itself, the old familiar form that first took shape four centuries ago. A laptop computer is a wondrous thing; it is inconceivable to me now that I ever did without one, particularly in writing and revision. (There are still, of course, those novelists who like to speak fervently of writing by hand in special lined journals, or using the old Royal typewriter they were given when they went away to Choate forty years before. Not me.) But a computer is no substitute for a book. No one wants to take a computer to bed at the end of a long day, to read a chapter or two before dropping off to sleep. No one wants to take one out of a purse on the New York City subway to pass the time between Ninety-sixth Street and the World Trade Center. No one wants to pass *Heidi* on disk down to their daughter on the occasion of her eighth birthday, or annotate William Carlos Williams on-screen. At least, no one wants to do it yet, even those who are much farther along the cybercurve than I am. The dis-ease Ms. Ellis felt reading a book on the computer, which she described so eloquently in her *Horn Book* article, is what so many of the rest of us feel, and why the book continues to prosper. Ms. Ellis wonders if this is generational, if she finds reading a screen less satisfactory than do children born to its blandishments. But I have three of those children, and while they play games, trade mail, and do plenty of research on their computers, they do most of their reading in plain old ordinary books, some that belonged to me years ago. They seem to like it that way. My youngest grew up with a copy of *Arthur's Teacher Trouble* on CD-ROM, an interactive version of the picture book that allowed her to use her mouse to make desks open and birds fly. But she never gave up reading the version on paper. "I like the real book," she said.

And a real book, not a virtual version, is more often than not what's wanted. After all, the publisher of Dutton Children's Books did not decide to publish *The End of the Rainbow* on-line because children were clamoring to read it on the computer. His reasons were financial, not philosophical; he simply did not believe he could afford the loss that the book would incur in conventional publication. The prophets of doom and gloom and the virtual library may use this to generalize about a future in which hundreds, perhaps thousands of wonderful books are never published at all. But the fact is that publishing in all its incarnations–small presses, large presses, vanity presses, university presses–produces many more new titles today than it did fifty or a hundred years ago. More than 350,000 new books were added to the Library of Congress in 1995 alone; that institution, founded with funding of $5000 two centuries ago, now has 200 times the number of items once found in the legendary library in Alexandria.

And if some new books only manage to make their way onto the Internet, isn't that better than losing them entirely? New technology offered the publisher of Dutton Children's Books, Christopher Franceschelli, some useful middle ground between taking a substantial financial loss and not offering the book to readers at all. He wrote eloquently in a letter to *The Horn Book*, "We live in an era of transition perhaps not all that dissimilar to that of five hundred years ago. Then an entire culture had to wrestle with the meaning of the Western re-invention of movable type. Even then there were those who bemoaned the loss of texture, when the individually crafted, individually illuminated manuscript, with rubricated initials and tooled leather bindings, gave way to the radically simple black and white pages mechanically produced by Gutenberg and his descendants. Indeed there are those who would argue that the entire Protestant movement was only possible once the Book had lost its totemic value as literal manifestation of the divine Word to reappear as the book–cheap, portable, with a mutable text accessible to (and interpretable by) one and all."

And in his history of reading, Albert Manguel concludes, "It is interesting to note how often a technological development-such as Gutenberg's promotes rather than eliminates that which it is supposed to supersede." Consider, for instance, the thousands of books sold every day on-line. In at least one way, those computer services that were said to spell *finis* to book buying in America have instead succeeded in making it easier for the technologically adept.

Katherine Paterson, in her library speech, took the long view, too, describing her despair at trying to find information on an on-line service and turning to an old encyclopedia and finding it there instead, but noting, too, "I think it well behooves us to realize that we are not the first generation to fear the changes that seem to engulf us. Plato, lest we forget, argued in the *Dialogues* that if people learned to read and write, poetry would disappear, for it was only in the oral tradition that poetry could be preserved properly."

Well, Plato was wrong. And so, I believe, are those people predicting the demise of the book, particularly its death by microchip. The discussions surrounding the issue always remind me of the discussions from my childhood about the gastronomic leap forward occasioned by the development of astronaut food. Soon, we heard, we would be able to eat an entire Sunday dinner in the form of a pill. Soon a Creamsicle could be carried around in your pocket, run under the hose, and reconstituted on a warm day, almost as good as new.

It's thirty years since man first walked on the moon, and when people sit down to a big old-fashioned supper it is still a plate of roast beef and mashed potatoes, not a capsule and a glass of water. When they buy a Creamsicle, it's three-dimensional, wet and cold and wonderful. That's because people like the thing itself. They don't eat mashed potatoes with gravy because they just need to be nourished, but because mashed potatoes and gravy are wonderful in so many ways: the heat, the texture, the silky slide of the gravy over your tongue. And that is the way it is with books. It is not simply that we need information, but that we want to savor it, carry it with us, feel the heft of it under our arm. We like the thing itself.

It is not possible that the book is over. Too many people love it so. It is possible that it has fallen upon hard times, but finding the evidence to prove this is more challenging than many people may think. It is true that there are almost no serializations of books in magazines anymore, a form of book that once made novels accessible for millions of readers who could not afford hardcovers. It is true that department stores no longer sell books, and that many of what pass for bookstores seem closer to gift shops, with far too many datebooks and trinkets. It's a little terrifying, the fact that in many of the mall stores there is an entire long wall classified as Fiction and a small narrow section to one side of it called Literature. That second, smaller, section is reserved largely for dead people, dead people who represent much of the best the world of words has had to offer over its long span.

But the ultimate truth is that they aren't dead, those people. The writers of books do not truly die; their characters, even the ones who throw themselves in front of trains or are killed in battle, come back to life over and over again. Books are the means to immortality: Plato lives forever, as do Dickens, and Dr. Seuss, Soames Forsyte, Jo March, Scrooge, Anna Karenina, and Vronsky. Over and over again Heathcliff wanders the moor searching for his Cathy. Over and over again Ahab fights the whale. Through them all we experience other times, other places, other lives. We manage to become much more than our own selves. The only dead are those who grow sere and shriveled within, unable to step outside their own lives and into those of others. Ignorance is death. A closed mind is a catafalque.

I still remember sitting in the fading afternoon one day in a rambling old house in the country speaking to the elderly matriarch of one of America's great publishing families, a woman known for her interest in all things political, social, intellectual. Near the end of our conversation she squared her shoulders, looked sharply into some middle distance behind me, and said, as though to herself, "I can't read any longer." The words were sad and sonorous as a church bell, and I felt that she had pronounced a sort of epitaph upon herself, and I felt that she felt it too: I can't read any longer.

Yet in her sorrow there was joy, the remembered joy of someone who had been a reader all her life, whose world had been immeasurably enlarged by the words of others. Perhaps it is true that at base we readers are dissatisfied people, yearning to be elsewhere, to live vicariously through words in a way we cannot live directly through life. Perhaps we are the world's great nomads, if only in our minds. I travel today in the way I once dreamed of traveling as a child. And the irony is that I don't care for it very much. I am the sort of person who prefers to stay at home, surrounded by family, friends, familiarity, books. This is what I like about traveling: the time on airplanes spent reading, solitary, happy. It turns out that when my younger self thought of taking wing, she wanted only to let her spirit soar. Books are the plane, and the train, and the road. They are the destination, and the journey. They are home.

J. Bathanti

Joseph Bathanti insists there is room for a laptop on his writing table. When asked about the baseball bat he says, "There's a lot of sports memorabilia (including a baseball on the far left side of the writing table nestled among photographs) all over my office. There are a number of bats and baseball gloves. I conflate baseball with Catholic."

J. McBreen

My best writing space is in Tuam and this is a picture of where I do my writing. The strange thing is that all the people who come to see me at our beautiful house in Connemara think that is where I write my best poems. In actual fact the intensity and sheer divine shape and colour and diversity of the views across the lakes, mountains and sea are far too distracting. I can barely concentrate on writing my emails!!

The late wonderful Irish writer, John McGahern, lived in a lovely part of County Leitrim and wrote at a table facing a blank wall. In Tuam it is not quite like that for me; my writing table, which is the family dining table, is set in the middle of our house facing out on my garden which is mature and colourful in all seasons but has high trees at the end of it blocking out the "beyond."

As I write this I suddenly realise that it is not from the "beyond" the true poetic imagination is nurtured but from the here and now.

— Joan McBreen

DAVID CROSBY

A busload of Hispanic students arrived for The Little Read festivities as David Crosby began shooting Julia Alvarez. "The bus parked behind me and she began calling out to them in Spanish," he recalls. "She called them over and they gathered around her, thrilled someone important spoke their language and wanted to talk to them."

25

Hickory-based photographer David Crosby hails from Lockport, NY. One of his favorite writers, Joyce Carol Oates, is also from Lockport. When he heard she was visiting Lenoir-Rhyne, he asked if he could photograph her. The University said yes, but her people declined. From that point forward, Visiting Writers Series' contracts require that writers consent to having their photos taken while at the University. Crosby has shot every writer since.

MARCH RENGA
Julia Alavarez

1

a haiku a day
might keep March doldrums away—
no harm in trying

2

Italian proverb
says that on the first of March
madmen go barefoot—

Sane Vermonters say:
keep your hat, coat, *and* boots on
till the first of May

3

watercolor light—
I glance at the calendar:
it's already March!

4

waking to birdsong—
robins, bluebirds, chickadees:
the song of their names.

5

on the snowy deck
where we dumped the Christmas tree—
sparrows caroling

6

old March wind blows hard—
must be trying to put out
a zillion candles

7

another snowstorm—
old nests filling with new snow,
bluebirds feeling blue

8

snow for days on end—
brown fields are white again
snow on the snowdrops

9

on the windowsill
paperwhites: indoor cousins
of snowflakes outside

10

during a cold snap
the pink amaryllis opens—
consolation prize

11

snow melting rivers
flooding sap running—the earth
giving at the seams

12

frozen lake thawing
dreaming again of living
a bigger-size life

13

baby gazing out
from father's back carrier:
her first spring ever

14

the old woman says
she can't get enough of spring—
her eyes, young, sky blue

15

the child asks why
are the eyes of March bad luck—
don't they see spring's back?

16

early crocuses
more incredibly purple
than I remember

17

in case I forgot—
after the long, hard winter:
crocuses, snowdrops

18

listen! what was that?
—whippoorwill or chickadee,
the song still pretty

19

birds feeling the urge,
feeling it, too, leading him
by the hand upstairs

20

so that's where it went!
—after the garden snowmelt
my long lost trowel

21

perennial beds—
I sure like the sound of that
now that I'm older.

22

high in the night sky
the big dipper pouring out
big servings of spring

23

geese are back, noisy
and full of themselves, having
been to Florida.

24

driving home from work—
sky still light enough to see
my neighbor waving

25

out in their front yards
first warm day of the season:
spring apparitions

26

first wash hung outside—
a pair of long underwear
kicking up its heels

27

neighborhood trash day:
big piles by each curbside—
spring cleaning booty

28

beside the new house,
a bird nest in the maple—
everyone cozy.

29

we're in for it now. . .
crocuses, wild violets
tulips, daffodils

30

suddenly wanting
to bow my head—not to pray
no, not exactly

31

a haiku a day
kept my March doldrums away—
onwards to April!

"March Renga," is part of a series I began around 2001, in which I set out
to write a poem about every month. I think I only got through April, then
jumped to November, and finally abandoned the project. It was a mis-
guided effort to take care of all my Christmas presents for that year, by
collecting them into a poetry calendar I intended to gift to everybody. Not
the best inducement for the muse, holiday shopping madness helpmeet!

—Julia Alvarez

WHOSE WOODS THESE ARE

Donald Secreast

Brought up in one of the poorest regions on Earth in the dim and diminished future, Peyton Gilley learned early that he was a lot more likely to find a friend with money than the money itself. Long before he followed his daddy into the small furniture factory thirty-five miles from the vinyl shack where they lived on a bare ridge overlooking the Goshen Creek Reservoir, wood had become a rare building material, more expensive than any of the remaining precious metals.

Only the wealthiest could afford furniture made out of real wood—even wood that had been recycled from other uses. Earth hadn't been able to sustain trees since before Peyton's daddy died, almost sixty years earlier. But he had taught Peyton everything that could be taught about working wood. Then Peyton taught himself a few tricks his daddy hadn't known. He had gotten good enough there in that small, dying factory to impress a few influential people who placed orders for special pieces of furniture, beds that cost enough to set up a small colony on the moon, chairs expensive enough to finance a modest supply depot on Mars, and a Bombay chest whose final price could have renovated five square city blocks in downtown Titan City.

For a while, Peyton made a good enough living. Not good enough that he could ever afford any of the wood furniture he sawed, sanded, carved, and assembled. But he did have rich friends. One pharmaceutical friend of Peyton exercised his authority when the life-extending drug, acetyl-chosteapsin, brand name, Geriaphage, became available to the public—the very rich public, naturally—and got Peyton on the list of pre-paid clients.

So, Peyton Gilley lived long after wood ceased completely to be available for furniture. When the factory closed, the last on the planet, Peyton retired to his family cabin and carved small animals from what was left of the wood scraps he had hoarded over the years. On special occasions, he would give the small animals to the children of influential people, thereby keeping himself fresh in the memories of the people whose generosity kept him alive.

He became a cultural treasure. By keeping in touch with the rich, Peyton one day found himself being informed that according to all the official records, he was the last artist of genuine wood alive in the solar system. Sometimes, when Peyton dreamed, he found himself back in the small factory, but instead of the carefully padded containers holding the reworked slats of recycled lumber, Peyton walked down aisles of handtrucks, high and heavy as elephants with freshly planed wood, especially pine, Peyton's favorite, because the smell made him feel like it was morning all day long.

Then, years after Peyton had run out of wood scraps, a whole planet of trees was discovered in the Epsilon Eridani system. Of course, they weren't trees like anybody had ever seen—although by this time only the very oldest of the very rich had lived long enough to have seen a real earth tree. Even Peyton felt confused by the first holographs that came back from the tree planet. They were huge like redwoods, but their trunks had a smooth look and a luster that didn't seem right to Peyton. And as it turned out, the entire planet seemed to grow only one species of tree.

A few days after the first holographs arrived from the tree planet, Peyton received an invitation to the governor's mansion. A shipment of lumber was on its way to earth, and several of the major solar system corporations wanted Peyton to make commemorative furniture. Certainly, Peyton wasn't aging nearly as fast as less treasured members of the population, but he wasn't getting any younger by a long shot.

They opened the factory back up, although except for the security guards, Peyton had the place pretty much to himself. The camera crew also made themselves at home. And about eighty young men and women from a government technical college arrived with the lumber. Now that the earth would have a steady supply of wood, the government wanted to make sure that Peyton had enough apprentices. Having been alone for the last ten years, Peyton appreciated the company. But not half as much as he appreciated the alien wood.

The settlers on the far away world had sawmilled the wood for Peyton. At first, he was troubled when he inspected the top plank on the stack of lumber. It didn't appear to have a grain to it. To work wood sensibly—much less carve it—a man had to see the grain. It was the map you followed to give the wood shape. By way of experiment, Peyton took a small scrap of the wood and ran his knife blade along the edge. His mind drifted for a second to the last animal he had carved from his last scrap of earth wood.

The moment this thought entered his head, he felt his hands tighten, and he watched the knife blade dip and glide without hesitation for a solid hour. His apprentices squeezed in around him while the camera crew swooped and zoomed around his hands. The hound dog that emerged from the scrap of wood wasn't exactly a perfect replica of that last dog Peyton had been thinking of. It was better. More real looking.

In some ways, Peyton was more amazed by his carving abilities than any of the apprentices or any of the camera crew. They thought he was just that good. He knew better. He'd carved that dog twenty or thirty times before he ran out of earth wood. His dogs had never looked so real or arrived so fast. As the canine figurine was handed around, Peyton waited for someone to accuse him of being a fraud. Yes, he had put the blade to the wood to start with, but somehow, the rest of the job had taken place completely outside of his control. Unlikely as it sounded, the wood had done the work. However, Peyton didn't know how to tell his admirers that they were being misled.

When Peyton started to work on the furniture, a hundred stately but comfortable rocking chairs, the wood again took over his skills. As soon as he began sawing out the rough slats for the arms, the backs, and the seats, once he got a clear picture of how the chair was supposed to look, he discovered that he had less and less trimming to do. If he happened to be under observation, either by the camera crew or by one of his apprentices, he found he had to do the work the way it was supposed to be done. But as soon as he assigned everyone their jobs in different parts of the factory, every piece of wood he touched took its shape from his mind.

On several occasions, he tried to fool the wood. He'd start out thinking about the rocking chairs, but as soon as the wood began shaping itself in his hands, he'd switch mental images and throw in a dog or a table top. The wood couldn't be deceived, though. And all his helpers and supporters were amazed by how quickly he could turn out the chairs' components.

More than once, during meals with his apprentices, Peyton asked them if they noticed anything peculiar about the wood. Of course, these young people had no basis for comparing the alien wood's behavior to earth wood's behavior. In fact, earth wood might seem even more unusual than the alien wood. It was infinitely harder to work with than the alien wood. Closely, Peyton watched the teleholo special that came out on his alien wood project. Even in close ups, his work seemed perfectly natural—though unusually fast. But, like his apprentices, nobody watching the programs had any way of knowing how much more slowly earth wood took shape.

Whether it was the work or the company, Peyton didn't know, but his days in the factory were the happiest he could remember. The more he worked on the rocking chairs, despite how the wood's behavior puzzled him, the more complete and fulfilled he felt. At night, when he strolled to the corner of the factory where an apartment had been built for him, Peyton did experience a little anxiety. He thought he should tell someone about how the wood took its shape from his mind rather than from his hands, but he wasn't so old that the foolishness of his idea wasn't obvious to him. One of the side effects of the Geriaphage was episodic paranoia, one of the symptoms that required doctors to discontinue the longevity treatments in some patients. Not even Peyton's late night doubts about the alien wood depressed him as much as the possibility of being dropped from the Geriaphage program.

Then, in the morning, one of his apprentices would bring him breakfast, and afterwards, they'd walk back to the brightly lit work area, where Peyton would pick up a piece of wood, and all his worries faded away. In fact, the more he worked with the wood, the more its oddness soothed and reassured him. Besides, instead of losing his mental acuity, a condition that most often accompanied the onset of the drug's paranoia, Peyton was convinced that his mind worked more clearly than it had in years. In particular, his memories came back to him more sharply than ever before. And his dreams had taken on a vividness that he had never experienced. He dreamed most often of walking through a fragrant forest of ancient earth trees. As he passed by them, they took on the shape and features of people he had known, people he had wanted to know. Always, they wanted to speak to him, but he couldn't stop long enough to let them speak. He had to keep moving through them. He had somewhere to go.

Much sooner than anyone expected, the one hundred rocking chairs were finished. Assuming it would probably be the only opportunity they'd have, Peyton and his apprentices tried out the chairs before calling in the security guards to help them crate up the chairs and send them off to their owners. As he eased himself back and forth, Peyton knew that the alien wood shifted its shape ever so slightly to accommodate the irregularities in his flesh and bones. Studying his apprentices with his practiced eye, he saw that each chair was changing its curves just a fraction of an inch here and there to relieve a pressure point or support a defective tissue of muscle.

From his apprentices' expressions, Peyton could tell that the chairs were so comfortable as to be therapeutic. The longer he sat in the chair, the stronger, younger, and more serene he felt. He remembered an ancient country song that his daddy used to sing to his mama, "Rolling in My Sweet Baby's Arms." The chair held him like the memory of that song, and its support along his back and hips, arms and thighs was now an embrace, taking him back to a time before he had to feed himself or carry himself around or be afraid, tired, hungry.

From what Peyton could gather after the guards came in about thirty minutes later and found him and his apprentices asleep in the chairs, all of them had the same dream, and it was Peyton's dream about walking in the forest. But the guards, in a hurry to get the chairs shipped to their influential owners, didn't give the wood workers time to draw any conclusions about their simultaneous nap and their identical dream. By this time, Peyton wasn't susceptible to a troubled state of mind.

In a matter of days, his apprentices were sent off to take charge of their own furniture factories, huge affairs. No one expected production levels to be measurable for a year or two. Workers had to be trained. However, to everyone's surprise—except the people who actually worked with the alien wood—all of the factories began shipping huge quantities of the rocking chairs within the first month of receiving the alien lumber. For a while, Peyton kept expecting a new set of specifications to come in for a different run of furniture. After all, how many rocking chairs did the world need? But all his factory kept making were rocking chairs.

After three years, every rich person in the solar system had a rocking chair, and prices dropped. After another three years, the factory workers were able to buy the chairs for themselves and all their family members. When Peyton wasn't supervising the effortless manufacturing of the chairs, he sat rocking in his own. After a while, he wasn't sure if he was eating regularly. It didn't seem as urgent a task as it once did. Irregular as his personal habits became, Peyton still believed his mind was clearer than it had ever been. His thoughts felt sharp-edged and articulated as individual leaves on a maple. Or as precise and distinct as pine needles. At night, memories and dreams rustled against his skull.

For ten years, production of the rocking chairs increased, with new factories springing up on every habitable planet. Still, no one, not even Peyton, felt any disappointment when the shipments from the alien world stopped coming in. The world had reached a saturation point, he figured. If anyone had been keeping count, he would have predicted that distribution was complete. One morning, everyone woke up, sitting in their rocking chairs, and shared a single awareness that they were entering a new season.

Through a window across the room from where he sat, Peyton could see that no one was moving any more than he was. It was the quietest he'd ever heard the world. But he didn't feel alone. In fact, he felt more connected to the rest of the world and all the people in it than he ever had. Deep as it grew, Peyton didn't have to work to establish this relationship. He didn't have to show anyone, rich or otherwise, what he could do for them. They all flowed together.

For one last time, Peyton opened his eyes and saw small leaves sprouting from the back of his hands. Sinking into the comfort of his alien wood rocking chair, he knew the truth. Everywhere in this world and others, the chairs were returning to the trees they had been for eons, taking their owners along. Cities and their technological wonders just so much fertilizer. It was an invasion Peyton knew he could happily live with for a long, long time.

BEACONS AT BEALTAINE

Seamus Heaney

In the Celtic calendar that once regulated the seasons in many parts of Europe, May Day, known in Irish as Bealtaine, was the feast of bright fire, the first of summer, one of the four great quarter days of the year. The early Irish Leabhar Gabhála (The Book of Invasions), tells us that the first magical inhabitants of the country, the Tuatha Dé Danaan, arrived on the feast of Bealtaine, and a ninth century text indicates that on the same day the druids drove flocks out to pasture between two bonfires. So there is something auspicious about the fact that a new flocking together of the old European nations happens on this day of mythic arrival in Ireland; and it is even more auspicious that we celebrate it in a park named after the mythic bird that represents the possibility of ongoing renewal. But there are those who say that the name Phoenix Park is derived from the Irish words, fionn uisce, meaning "clear water" and that coincidence of language gave me the idea for this poem. It's what the poet Horace might have called a carmen sæculare, a poem to salute and celebrate an historic turn in the sæculum, the age.

BEACONS AT BEALTAINE
Phoenix Park, May Day, 2004

Uisce: water. And fionn: the water's clear.
But dip and find this Gaelic water Greek:
A phoenix flames upon fionn uisce here.

Strangers were barbaroi to the Greek ear.
Now let the heirs of all who could not speak
The language, whose ba-babbling was unclear,

Come with their gift of tongues past each frontier
And find the answering voices that they seek
As fionn and uisce answer phoenix here.

The May Day hills were burning, far and near,
When our land's first footers beached boats in the creek
In uisce, fionn, strange words that soon grew clear;

So on a day when newcomers appear
Let it be a homecoming and let us speak
The unstrange word, as it behoves us here,

Move lips, move minds and make new meanings flare
Like ancient beacons signalling, peak to peak,
From middle sea to north sea, shining clear
As phoenix flame upon fionn uisce here.

Seamus Heaney's office,

Dublin, IRELAND

FINDING LOUISE

Josephine Humphreys

I used to think writing and typing were pretty much the same thing. Make an outline, type your way through it with topic sentences, logically developed paragraphs, good grammar, and you're a writer. This way you keep your guard up against the chaos of the whirling mind, Miss Harriet Wilson told me in the eighth grade, and the method lasted me all the way through graduate school and almost a decade of teaching. But when I started to write fiction at the age of 33, I had to unlearn my method. It was missing something. Or more accurately, it was blocking something, that mysterious contribution that may come unbidden into the writer's consciousness from somewhere deeper than logic and reason, maybe directly from the whirling chaos. Typing is necessary, and logic helps out along the way, but I've learned to let my guard down. I wait for the uninvited, and if it comes I let it in. Then something happens that I do not orchestrate and must not try to control. There will be surprise and discovery, maybe even revelation. Occasionally, when I'm lucky, there is transformation.

The steps in my revised method are simple: sit down at the desk, type, and see what comes out. No outline.

One such transformation occurred while I was beginning to write *Rich in Love*, my second novel. I sat and typed, and out came Lucille Odom, riding her bicycle home from school. I followed. I listened when she talked. And one day, describing the kind of girl she had been, she said something that completely surprised me.

"I liked history," she said.

But I myself had never had an interest in history. There was too much of it around me in my town, Charleston, S.C., and most of it had to do with war. In college I side-stepped the history requirement by taking economics as an allowable alternative. History struck me as dead and buried and boring. But here was Lucille suddenly explaining to me why I was wrong. "I liked history. Not the kind in the textbooks, the treaties and political parties and government shenanigans, all of which gave me a headache. There was more to history than that. There were things hidden in it, mysteries worth going after."

She convinced and converted me.

I suppose it's easiest to understand this as my own subconscious rising through the voice of my fictional character, revealing ideas that simply hadn't surfaced before. Or you could call it a form of inspiration. At any rate, the message was valuable, even crucial at the time, because for many years I'd been hopelessly dreaming of a book I wanted to write but thought I couldn't – because it was based on a true story of the South during Reconstruction, and would therefore have to be a historical novel. If I knew no history, how could I write a historical novel? But Lucille Odom's message changed me from someone who'd never seen any point in digging up the past into someone eager to unearth history's treasures. And I knew which mystery I wanted to dig for. I'd first heard about it when I was seventeen years old, on a train ride from Charleston to Boston, going to see a boy.

At seventeen, I had two things on my mind: words and boys. I loved them both, with about equal fervor. I read books like a fiend and took them to heart; I daydreamed about boys and found them dangerously fascinating. In my diary, the New Year's resolutions I had recorded were "Get more books" and "Get more boys."

Books were easy to get. But you can't go down to the library and take a boy out on loan. I was a shy girl, with no idea of how to flirt with boys, or even how to talk to them. I'd managed to attract the interest of the one in Boston by writing letters to him for nearly a year, and finally he had invited me to a college dance. In retrospect I've often suspected that my early interest in writing was a compensation for my lack of chatting talent. Writing was always easier than talking. Even with girls I had trouble making conversation. I couldn't confide the way you're supposed to with your closest pal. My female friends were all paired off in twos, leaving me as the only one without a best friend.

Of the larger world I actually knew very little, but I was under the impression that I knew everything. I was a "good girl," a straight-A student, a listener and observer, in love with my home and my family and, to some degree, myself. I thought I understood both the person I was and the universe I inhabited. I wanted to be a writer, and Miss Wilson had told me I might get to be one. My grandmother thought so too, and hadn't the Boston boy had liked my letters?

Near Lumberton, N.C., the train stopped for new passengers. A girl my age got on, wearing a white cotton dress with a matching bolero jacket, carrying a bunch of flowers. Behind her followed a young blond sailor in white, his cap pushed back. The girl plopped down in the empty seat next to me while the sailor went on up to the first seat in the car.

"Do you mind if I sit here?" she asked me. "We just got married but we're having our first fight and I don't want to talk to him."

She was the prettiest girl I'd ever seen, with long dark hair and unusual eyes. I couldn't decide what to call their color. Greenish brown with flecks of gold. I moved my bags to give her room.

"He's making me go meet his parents in Rhode Island," she said. "But I know they won't like me."

I couldn't imagine anyone not liking this person. Not only did she have the looks of a movie star, but she had that boldness I lacked, the daring, confident charm that would let her strike up conversations with strangers, and tell them her secrets. I was entranced.

"Why wouldn't they like you?" I asked.

"Because they're white. And I'm not."

In the segregated city where I grew up, racial identity was a simple matter. Everyone was either black or white. There were no other possibilities, even when other possibilities seemed more probable. An old Asian man who farmed strawberries was a puzzle to everyone for a while until it was decided he was black, since he had black children. One family in town was understood to be "not strictly white" but certainly not black, so they were white. As for Indians, I'd heard of people having a Cherokee great-grand-mother, but I'd been told the real Indians had "died out." From time to time I questioned Jim Crow segregation and got into some arguments with family members, but I never once questioned the racial categories themselves. That was the way it was. You were black or you were white.

So I couldn't understand what she had just said. I was looking at her, and I saw a white girl.

"Then what are you?" I blurted.

"Lumbee Indian," she said.

"What's that?"

I knew my questions were rude. But I don't regret asking, even now almost fifty years later, because her answer set me on a path that would change my life, change my way of thinking, change me. For the next hour she talked about the Lumbee people of North Carolina and their legendary hero, the outlaw Henry Lowrie. All of it was new to me. I was especially struck by what she told me of Henry's wife, Rhoda, and her role as the outlaw's sweetheart. Who were these people? Why had I not heard of them before? Who was this bride who could sweep me away with the telling of a hundred-year-old tale? I knew right then that if I could ever become a writer, this outlaw story was the book I'd want to write. In the very same instant I knew I wouldn't, because I had already closed the door on history.

I didn't try to open that door until after Lucille Odom converted me, long after the chance to take history courses was over. I had to make my own syllabus. At first I found very little published information about Henry Lowrie and the Lumbees, and nothing about Rhoda. The Lumbees still lived in Robeson County, just over the North Carolina state line, but few South Carolinians had ever heard of them, and in their home state they were generally ignored or maligned. During the decade following the Civil War, Henry had been outlawed for leading a band of young Lumbee men in revolt against the powers that were, embarking on a string of robberies and killings after witnessing the lynching of his father and brother. He was daring and handsome, laconic, by some accounts a man of honor, by others a cold-blooded killer. In spite of a huge reward offered by the state, no one ever turned him in. He simply disappeared. There were rumors – he'd shot himself, on purpose or by accident; or been killed by his brother; or escaped to Tennessee (or California or Mexico) and started a new life. Some said he came back in disguise from time to time. But there was no proof for any of these theories. His fate was a mystery. And the Lumbees themselves were regarded by their neighbors as a mystery, their origins undocumented. One historian suggested they might be the descendants of Walter Raleigh's early colonists on the North Carolina shore, and could have survived by moving inland and living among local Indian tribes.

I thought I might solve these mysteries.

So I read history for more than ten years, writing little pieces of the story now and then but wanting to store up as much research as I could, immerse myself in the past so that when I came to write in earnest, the facts would be in my head, and I could tell the story as if I were there by Henry's side – in a sense, as if I were Rhoda. I dug through courthouse documents and libraries, poring over old newspapers, letters, memoirs, and maps. To understand Reconstruction I had to go back and learn about the Civil War, which in turn required me to study Antebellum history and even the American Revolution and Colonial period, following threads of the Lumbee story back as far as I could.

Meanwhile I was writing and publishing other things, contemporary stories about Southern families in various sorts of distress. But Henry and Rhoda lurked behind every one of them. In my mind Henry was the ultimate Boy, fascinating and dangerous, and Rhoda was the girl on the train, telling her story. I began peppering my books with tiny secret notes to myself, reminders of the unwritten, maybe unwriteable, novel that had come to obsess me.

In *Rich in Love*, for instance, I used a Lumbee surname, Oxendine, for one of the characters. It was just a little memo to myself, a hidden signal that nobody else would understand or even notice.

One day at the invitation of a Durham book club, I drove up to North Carolina to give a little talk about fiction-writing. I love Southern women's book clubs. We had a pleasant lunch; I talked about my published novels, answered questions and signed some books and ate some brownies. I was about to leave when one of the members, a tiny pretty woman about my age came up to me and introduced herself as Louise Maynor.

"I was just wondering why you used the name Oxendine in *Rich in Love*," she said.

"Oh—well, it's a Lumbee Indian name."

"Yes, I know," she said. "But why did you use it?"

I caught my breath and for the first time confessed my obsession. "I've always wanted to write the story of Henry and Rhoda Lowrie."

Louise smiled. "If you do," she said, "will Henderson Oxendine be one of your characters?"

"He's my favorite!"

So she knew the story. She knew that Henderson had been one of Henry's cousins and a member of the outlaw gang, known for his mild-mannered ways and his singing voice. In fact he sang at his own hanging in 1872, convicted of a murder he didn't commit. A sketch of him had been published in the *New York Herald* that year, showing a thin handsome young man who reminded me of my own father.

"I'm glad you're going to include him," Louise said. "He was my great-grandfather."

She was only the second Lumbee I had met, after the girl on the train, and I was excited to make the connection. But what really shot through me like fire was a sudden understanding that the story of Henry Lowrie and Rhoda Strong and Henderson Oxendine was not dead and buried. It was continuing. I'd never imagined that one day I would stand face to face with the living descendant of one of the characters occupying my head.

Louise was the first I met, but others followed, and the line between past and present became a moveable boundary.

Without question, I could never have written *Nowhere Else on Earth* without Louise's help. After the Durham book club meeting, we went out for a cup of coffee that lasted all afternoon. We discovered that her daughter and my son were the same age—and were headed for the same college that fall. We laughed at the same things and had voted for the same candidates, and when we finally said our good-byes, we agreed to get together again. We did, soon and often. Louise would eventually invite me many times to the Lumbee town of Pembroke where she had grown up and where the annual Lumbee Homecoming takes place, a 4th of July weekend celebration when all Lumbees are supposed to come home for parades, family reunions, beauty contests, and general festivity. Through her I got to know the town and the countryside, her family and friends. Best of all, I got to know Louise herself.

She urged me on. Whenever I got discouraged, she encouraged. One time I told her I feared I was just a "wannabe," an outsider who shouldn't even be attempting to write the story of a people who weren't my own.

"You're not a wannabe," she said in her soft, gentle voice. "You're a wewantchatobe."

I've never met a more generous, cheerful, witty, gracious person.

When I re-created Rhoda Lowrie as a fictional character, I drew from several different real-life people. There's the historical Rhoda, whom I knew only in a blurry form from a few paragraphs in newspapers and memoirs of her day. There's also a good bit of myself, discernible maybe in the fictional Rhoda's lonesomeness and dreams. And there's the girl on the train, with her bold courage and her charm. But in ways that aren't obvious except to me, at Rhoda's heart there is Louise's strength, Louise's hope and determination and curiosity and wisdom, Louise's love.

Ordinarily after I finish a novel I almost forget that it exists. I don't return to it. But that's not the case with *Nowhere Else on Earth*. I'm still in touch with friends in Pembroke, and I still read everything I can find about Lumbee history. As for Louise – I no longer think of her as my connection to the Lumbees, or as Henderson Oxendine's great-granddaughter, or as a model for the character of Rhoda. She is astronomically more. We recently spent a getaway week together in North Carolina where we laughed ourselves silly, cried some, confided our latest joys and worries. I can say of Louise the same thing Rhoda says of her friend Margaret in *Nowhere Else on Earth* – that she's the best friend I could have found for myself, because we have the same dream of life. She is Rhoda's gift to me.

The Confederate Home was a home for widows of Civil War soldiers. I believe it's one of only two such buildings left in the South. Today the Charleston home is a residence for elderly women, but it also has some studio space for writers and artists. I'm lucky to have an incredible little room with big windows and a lovely view. Now and then I tape some kind of mysterious picture onto the curtain – this one is a 19th-century industrial site somewhere in Virginia. I just thought it was strange and beautiful.

—Jo Humphreys

came back. With Irene's silences, he had felt isolated, left out,
wondering what of it, if anything, was his fault. Now, Joe Pike's
preoccupation with the motorcycle gave him the same old spooked
feeling. Joe Pike, like Irene, seemed

decide...

From

DAIRY QUEEN DAYS

By Robert Inman

CHAPTER ONE

when his father, Reverend

e motorcycle. Maybe even
her off to the Institute. But
ng that unpleasantness
m, as they said -- until he

nce been a
d brought it
tchen window
the garage
e, Joe Pike had
ed, staring at the

ROBERT INMAN

From

DAIRY QUEEN DAYS

Robert Inman

Trout Moseley was a day shy of sixteen when his father, Reverend Joe Pike Moseley, ran away.

Most people thought it started with the motorcycle. Maybe even before that, when they sent Trout's mother off to the Institute. But people thought Joe Pike had been handling that unpleasantness reasonably well — keeping his equilibrium, as they said — until he showed up with the motorcycle.

It was an ancient Triumph, or at least what had once been a Triumph. Joe Pike found it in a farmer's barn, in pieces, and brought it home in the trunk of his car. Trout was standing at the kitchen window when he saw Joe Pike back the car down the driveway to the garage behind the parsonage. By the time Trout got out there, Joe Pike had the trunk open and was standing with his arms crossed, staring at the jumble of wheel rims, pitted chrome pieces, engine, handlebars, gasoline tank.

"What's that?" Trout asked.

"A once and future motorcycle."

"What're you gonna do with it?"

Joe Pike uncrossed his arms and hitched up his pants from their accustomed place below his paunch. "Fix it up. I am the resurrection and the life. Yea, verily." A trace of a smile played at his lips. *"Up from the grave he arose!"* he sang off-key. Joe Pike sang badly, but enthusiastically. In church, he could make the choir director wince. He referred to his singing as "making a joyful noise."

"You know anything about motorcycles?" Trout asked.

"Not much."

"Need some help?"

Joe Pike stared for a long time at the jumble of metal in the trunk of the car. Trout wondered after awhile if he had heard the question. Then finally Joe Pike said, "I reckon I can manage. It ain't heavy."

"I mean..." But then he saw that Joe Pike wasn't really paying him any attention. His mind was there inside the trunk among the parts of the old Triumph, perhaps deep down inside one of the cylinders of the engine, imagining a million tiny explosions going off rapid-fire. Trout studied him for a minute or so, then shrugged and turned to go.

"It's a four-cycle," Joe Pike said.

Trout turned and looked at him again. Joe Pike's gaze never left the motorcycle. "What?"

"You don't have to mix the gas and oil."

"That's good," Trout said. "You might forget."

When Trout looked out the kitchen window again a half-hour later, the trunk of the car was closed and so were the double doors of the old wood-frame garage. But he could faintly hear Joe Pike singing inside, *"Rescue the perishing, care for the dying!"*

Over the next two months, Trout stayed away from the garage when Joe Pike was out there. But he followed the progress of the motorcycle by sneaking a look when Joe Pike was gone. At first it was a spindly metal frame propped on two concrete blocks like a huge insect, and metal parts bobbing like apples in a ten-gallon galvanized washtub filled with solvent to eat away years of grime and rust. Before long, with the metal sanded smooth, the motorcycle began to take shape on the frame. Joe Pike took the fenders, wheel rims, gasoline tank and handlebars to a body shop and had them re-painted and re-chromed. Replacement parts — headlamp, cables, speedometer — began to arrive by UPS.

Trout remained vaguely hopeful at first. Fifteen years old, almost sixteen, fascinated by the thought of motorized transportation. But he came to realize that Joe Pike had no intention of sharing the motorcycle.

Joe Pike worked on it in the garage deep into the night, showing up for breakfast bleary-eyed, smelling of grease and solvent, grime caked thick under his fingernails. That was uncharacteristic. Joe Pike was by habit a fastidious man. He took at least two baths a day — more in the summer, because he was a prodigious perspirer — and changed his underwear each time. But this present grubbiness didn't seem to bother him. Neither did the state of their housekeeping, which got progressively worse. The church had hired a cleaning woman to come once a week after Trout's mother went off to the Institute, but she was no match for the growing piles of dirty dishes and laundry. Trout finally took matters into his own hands and learned to operate the dishwasher and the washing machine and dryer. After a fashion. At school, he endured locker room snickers over underwear dyed pale pink by washing with a red tee-shirt. Joe Pike's underwear was likewise pale pink, but he didn't seem to notice, or at least he didn't remark upon it. Joe Pike's mind seemed to be fixed on the motorcycle, or whatever larger thing it was that the motorcycle represented. There was a gently stubborn set to his jaw, almost a grimness there. On Sundays his sermons were vague, rambling things, trailing off in mid-sentence. He didn't seem to be paying the sermons much attention, either. In the pews, members of the congregation would steal glances at each other, perplexed. *What?*

"How's it going?" Trout would ask.

"Okay."

"Don't you get cold out there?" It was March, the pecan trees in the parsonage yard still bare-limbed and gaunt against the gray morning sky.

A blank look from Joe Pike. "No. I reckon not." Then he would stare out the kitchen window in the direction of the garage and Trout would know that Joe Pike wasn't really there with him at all. He was out there with the Triumph.

It worried Trout a good deal for awhile. It brought back all the old business of his mother's long silences, the way she went away somewhere that nobody else could go, stayed for days at a time, and finally just never came back. With Irene's silences, he had felt isolated, left out, wondering what of it, if anything, was his fault. Now, Joe Pike's preoccupation with the motorcycle gave him the same old spooked feeling. Joe Pike, like Irene, seemed unreachable. And Trout finally decided there was really nothing he could do but watch and wait.

So he did, and so did the good people of Ohatchee, Georgia — particularly, the good people of Ohatchee Methodist. They watched, waited, talked:

"What you reckon he's gone do with that thing?"

"Give it to Trout, prob'ly. Man of his size'd bust the tires." (Hearty chuckle here. Joe Pike's stood six-feet-four and his weight ranged from 250 to 300 pounds, depending on whether he was in one of his Dairy Queen phases.)

"Well, it gives the Baptists something to talk about."

"Yeah. That and all the other."

"Damn shame."

"Was she hittin' the bottle?"

"Don't think so. Just went off the deep end."

"Poor old Joe Pike. And little Trout. Bless his heart."

Long pause. "Don't reckon Joe Pike had anything to do with it, do you?"

"'Course not." Longer pause. "But it does make you wonder."

"Reckon they'll transfer Joe Pike at annual conference?"

"Prob'ly not. He's only been here two years."

"Hmmm. But folks sure do talk."

"Yeah. 'Specially Baptists."

They talked among themselves, but they did not talk to Joe Pike Moseley about his motorcycle. No matter how gracefully he seemed to have handled the business of his wife, there was in general an air of disaster about Joe Pike. People were wary, as if he might be contagious. Then too, a motorcycle just didn't seem to be the kind of thing you discussed with a preacher. At least it didn't until Easter Sunday.

Ohatchee Methodist was packed, the usual crowd swelled by the once-a-year attendees, the ones Joe Pike referred to as "tourists." They were crammed seersucker-to-crinoline into the oak pews and in folding chairs set up along the aisles and the back wall. It was mid-April, already warm but not quite warm enough for air conditioning, so the windows of the sanctuary were open to the spring morning outside and the ceiling fans went *whoosh-whoosh* overhead, stirring the smell of new clothes and store-bought fragrances into a rich sweet stew.

When they were finally settled into their seats, the choir entered from the narthex singing, *"Up From the Grave He Arose!"* They marched smartly two-by-two down the aisle, proclaiming triumph o'er the grave, and the congregation rose with a flurry and joined in, swelling the high-ceiling sanctuary with their earnestness. The choir paraded up into the choir loft and everybody sang another verse and then they all sat down and stared at the door to the Pastor's Study to the right of the altar, expecting Joe Pike to emerge as was his custom. They sat there for a good while. Nothing. They began to look about at each other. *What?* Then after a minute or two, they heard the throaty roar of the motorcycle, faintly at first and then growing louder as it approached the church and stopped finally at the curb outside. Trout — seated midway in the middle section with his friend Parks Belton and Parks' mother Imogene — looked about for a route of discreet escape. Joe Pike had spent all night in the garage. He was still there when Trout left for Sunday School. And now he had ridden the motorcycle to church. *Maybe if I crawl under the pew.* But he sat there, transfixed. They were all transfixed.

After a moment, the swinging doors that separated the sanctuary from the narthex flew open and Joe Pike swept in, huge and hurrying, his black robe billowing about him, down the aisle and up to the pulpit. He stopped, looked out over the congregation, gave them all a vague half-smile, and then settled himself in the high-backed chair behind the pulpit. He slouched, one elbow propped on the arm of the chair, chin resting in his hand, one ham-like thigh hiked over the other, revealing a pair of scuffed brown cowboy boots. Trout stared at the boots. Joe Pike had bought them in Dallas years ago when he played football at Texas A&M, but they had been gathering dust in various parsonage closets for as long as Trout could remember. He had never seen Joe Pike wear the boots before.

The choir director, seated at the piano, gave Joe Pike a long look over the tops of her glasses. Then she nodded to the choir and they stood and launched into *"The Old Rugged Cross."* As they sang, Joe Pike sat staring out the window, the toe of his boot swaying slightly in time to the music, brow wrinkled in thought.

The last notes faded and the choir sat back down. Joe Pike remained in his seat, still staring out the window, out where the motorcycle was. The choir director gave an impatient cough. Then Joe Pike looked up, shook himself. He stood slowly and moved the two steps to the pulpit. He picked up the pulpit Bible. It was a huge thing, leather-bound with gold letters and gold edging and a long red ribbon to mark your place. Joe Pike held it in his left hand as if it weighed no more than a feather. He opened it with his right, flipped a few pages, found his place, marked it with his index finger.

His eyes searched the words for a long time. Then his brow furrowed in dismay, as if someone had substituted a Bible written in a foreign tongue. He looked up, gaze sweeping the congregation. His mouth opened, but nothing came out. Sweat beads began to pop out on his forehead. He opened his mouth again, made a little hissing sound through his teeth.

Trout had known for a good while that Joe Pike was really two people — the big man you saw and another, smaller one who was tucked away somewhere inside. Trout didn't know who the small man was. Maybe Joe Pike didn't either, actually. But he gave little evidences of himself in tiny movements of eye, hand, mouth — such as this business of hissing through the teeth — mostly when agitated. You had to be quick to catch it. Most people didn't. But Trout had formed the habit of watchfulness. You had to be watchful in a house where your mother said nothing for long stretches and your father was two people. So now, watching Joe Pike carefully, he saw this hissing through the teeth and read it as trouble, pure and simple.

"What's he doing?" Parks Belton whispered to Trout.

Trout shrugged. "I don't know."

Imogene Belton glared at them. "Shhhhhh!"

Suddenly, Trout felt a great urge to get up from his pew, go up to the pulpit and take the Bible from his father's hand, take him by the arm and say, "It's all right." He felt that the entire congregation, every last one of them, expected him to do just that. But he sat, as immobilized as the rest, all of them like morbid onlookers at the scene of a wreck. Finally, Joe Pike gave a great shuddering sigh and put the Bible back down.

There was a long, fascinated silence, a great holding of breath, broken only by the throb of the ceiling fans. And then Reverend Joe Pike Moseley said, "I'm sorry. I've got to go."

He closed the Bible with a thump. He drew in a deep breath. Then he walked quickly down from the pulpit and up the aisle, the black robe flapping about him, and out the door, looking neither left nor right. Not a soul inside the church moved. After a moment they heard the motorcycle cough to life out front. Joe Pike gunned it a couple of times, then dropped it into gear and roared away. They could hear him for a long time, until the sound finally faded as he topped the rise at the edge of town, heading west. They sat there for awhile longer and then one of the ushers got up and went through the swinging doors into the narthex. He returned, holding Joe Pike's black robe. "I reckon he's gone for the day," the man said. With that, everybody got up and went home.

THE WRITING LIFE
Dori Sanders

The mid-summer harvest season nearly always ushers in dry hot days — days that slowly merge into weeks, months and stack on top of one another as the calendar pushes the harvest season to its end.

The lay of the land before me is stuck in its seasonal mode — trees, undergrowth, grasses, weeds and the occasional blooming trumpet vines. In the distance, kudzu vines transform trees into towering sculptures. A work of art.

The view makes my thoughts revisit an earlier time, around 1915, when my father, a rural elementary school principal settled with his parents on their own farmland in Filbert, a small village in York County, South Carolina.

Now, with increased acreage and careful attention to fallow land and crop rotation, the same land has continued down through generations — fertile land for farming, still bringing forth bountiful crops of peaches and produce.

Farming is a way of life for me. I open my days early. Before the light of dawn. A great time to listen to the quiet and help gather freshly picked peaches and produce for the customers who visit our open-air peach shed on Highway 321.

Daily customers come and go, sharing stories of happiness and sadness, recipes and local news.

The farming life is not easy. Farming is hard physical work. So mundane, yet in some ways appealing. It's a work that allows the mind to be free. Free to listen to the faint roar of tractors in the din, the muted voices and laughter of workers in the fields and orchards... free to watch traffic flow up and down on the busy highway.

It was there I saw two passing funeral processions. Each with the usual

When the New York Times wrote, "'Clover' is very much the genuine item." Sanders said, "Of course it is! I just write what I hear. The banter at my farm stand serves as a well-spring of inspiration."

procedure for the area: a slow moving county police car with blue flashing lights followed by a hearse, family car, and then a line of mourners in cars with their lights turned on. Approaching vehicles slowed to a complete stop on the opposite side of the highway.

From all I could see in the first funeral procession, every person was African American. I watched, thinking I might know someone. I did not recognize a single soul. From one of the cars, a little girl waved to me from an open window. I watched her little cupped hand and it seemed as if she was trying to scoop sadness from the very air. I waved back to her.

I was sad.

Later the same day, there was yet another passing funeral procession with the same procedure.

And as far as I could see, everyone was white. Again, the long line of cars slowed to a complete stop.

In a car, right at the driveway to our peach shed, through an opened window I watched a young white woman cry. Watched her wipe away tears with a white lace handkerchief. I shared her sadness and wiped away my tears with the back of my hand.

I thought about death, so universal. So common to all. No matter who you are — no matter what color of skin you may have; rich or poor — you will learn about death. My thoughts stayed with the little girl with whom I also shared a sadness. Wondered what her life would be like if by chance she wound up with the white woman and the two of them ended up together on a peach farm in South Carolina. I wondered if they could make a life together. Learn to like each other. My imagination soared — *What if? What if?*

That observation was the basis for my first novel *Clover*, a story narrated by a ten-year-old little girl telling about her life with a white stepmother after the tragic death of her father, an African American school principal.

The wonderful daily flow of conversations that would go on and on at the peach shed served as the well-spring for my writing. Like a sponge, I soaked up all the banter and piece by piece sewed them together into my fictional quilt. My customers became my fictional characters.

So often in my writing I draw on the familial background of my youth. Childhood can only be interpreted when seen from the distance of years, and usually by that time few tangible reminders are left. For me, a rusting water tank atop a decaying cedar wood tower is all that remains of a sophisticated irrigation system that my father designed and built for watering the beds of sweet potato plants for our use and for sale. All this before we had electricity on the farm.

So many other things, like our old family home, remain intact in memory, yet in reality lie in ruin today. Old silent foundation stones are all that remain of a house that no longer stands. A home that now looms far nobler in decay then when it was new; an unattainable piece of the past becomes even more desirable because of its unattainability.

Happy, pleasant years now lost in memory. But all was not wonderful. Down through the years sadness has played a somber hand. While we mourn the death of relatives, we try to come to handle it. Mourning begins a long journey, an ever present sadness that cannot be ignored.

So even in my writing, I find, all in all, the farming life has brought its own satisfaction. It is the only thing that seems constant from generation to generation. There is that communality of soul between us farmers that is to this day ever-binding. Large farms or small, come springtime the talk of planting is common to us all.

I remember reading in one of Vincent Van Gogh's many letters to his brother Theo, "Don't let's forget that the little emotions are the great captions of our lives, and that we obey them without knowing it."

So lest the very vestige of the little things in my life all be washed away like the erosion of fine soil, I will doubtless continue to write to establish — if only in fiction — some permanence to it all.

64

PART TWO

Robert Hedin

TORNADO

Robert Hedin

Four farms over it looked like a braid of black hemp
I could pull and make the whole sky ring.
And I remember there falling to earth that night
The broken slats of a barn, baling wire, straw and hay,
And one black leather Bible with a broken spine.

I think of the bulls my father slaughtered every August,
How he would pull out of that rank sea
A pair of collapsed lungs, stomach,
Eight bushels of gleaming rope he called intestines,
And one bucket of parts he could never name.

In the dream that keeps circling back in the shape
Of a barn, my father has just drained
His last bull. Outside it is raining harder
Than I've ever seen, and the sky is about to step down
On one leg. And all through the barn,
As high as the loft, the smell of blood and hay.
All night, as long as the dream holds,
He keeps turning the thick slab of soap over and over,
Building the lather up like clouds in his hands.

ALL I COULD SEE I NAMED DARKNESS

Rhett Iseman Trull

Until
       you, lit, tapped me
on the shoulder the night
of Kari's party—Kari, lost
among her entourage, and me
on the periphery, thinking
I might slip the scene without
notice, as always. But then,
as the man whose parents
let him rename himself Flash
gunned his motorcycle to wheel
the fair Kari away and leave me
friendless, you introduced
yourself, as if all evening you'd been waiting
for the moment the beautiful crowd might
part and there I'd be.
               I'd thought
myself invisible, self-exiled
to the edges. All summer, come midnight,
I'd been sulking the streets,
apartments illumined where something was
happening: a couple kissing, curtains
undrawn; or a phone announcing
its call—surely, from someone's new
crush; someone, it seemed,

for everyone but me, spinster
already, wick never
fired. I figured this was the
life for me, like it or not: voyeur
of the neighborhood, popcorn
dinner for one, one
wine glass wearing a ring of red
in the sink. At least I could do
as I thought I pleased: stay out
until the bars flicked
off the music, on the lights;
let the tattoo artist
christen me with his needle—
on my shoulder, a wolf
howling with such longing I thought
its moon absent
until
      you stepped under
the patio lights and all the shadows
of the city
      shifted.

SONG FOR OUR BULLY

Rhett Iseman Trull

Again with her dark
        design, pretense of concern, she

gathers us, collecting this time our locker
        combinations, lest

we forget. She doesn't care. She never
        cared. She steals our hearts

to break them. But in harmony
        that comforts us, we

deliver: 13, 9, 22, right left right and
        open. And I say, Forgive her. Picture

the muddy spirits of her
        childhood, shapeless

barren years that shaped her: brother tied to
        morphine down the hall; a mother

rocking, in her rocker, gulleys
        in the carpet; hour

by hour, shadows heisting
        larger portions of the light. I knew her

then, before she learned to hide
	herself. Inevitable Monopoly

banker and victor, she offered me once her red hotels
	when I cried at the margin

of my loss. We fell asleep holding
	hands, woke not knowing whose

belonged to whom. When a boy, mouth
	an angry shine of braces, stole

my locket off its chain, she
	broke his nose to get it

back, pressed hard to my breast
	its oval of secrets, demanding,

Guard it, bruise over my heart beginning.

	She pretends now not to notice
me, but don't be fooled. Memory, the one vault

	she can't crack, presides. She knows
I know. She can't reverse the *we*

	we were. Can you see
her as I've seen her? See her mine

the radio for its sad songs: *exchange*
a walk on part in the war for a lead role

in a cage. See her by the creek, alone,
burying small objects: onyx brooch

her father sent, tooth
the fairy never came in the night

to switch for coin. Love.
Love her as I've loved her steeled

heart, concealing fracture. Sorry
some day, she will shatter. Today is just

her dumb brave act of translation:
from her pain she makes a music of our

cries. Ah, sweet demented
conductor. And generous—dividing

her burdens among us like wealth.

Rhett Iseman Trull

Robert Hedin's office

"Charm is definitely a part of my writing space. She loves it when I write because that means I'm going to be still and settled for hours. She gets in my lap and purrs and purrs, often with a book or notebook resting on top of her."

—Rhett Iseman Trull

75

THE WOMAN AT THE POND
Ron Rash

Water has its own archeology, not a layering but a leveling, and thus truer to our own sense of the past, because what is memory but near and far events spread and smoothed beneath the present's surface. A green birthday candle that didn't expire with a wish lies next to a green lantern lit twelve years later. Chalky sun-motes in a sixth-grade classroom harbor close to a university library's high window, a song on a staticy radio shoals against the same song at a hastily arranged wedding reception. This is what I think of when I hear James Murray's daughter has decided to drain the pond. A fear of lawsuits, she claims, something her late father considered himself exonerated from by a sign warning *Fish And Swim At Your Own Risk.*

Wallace Rudisell is the man hired to the job, a task that requires opening the release valve on the standpipe, then keeping it clear until what once was a creek will be a creek once more. I grew up with Wallace, and, unlike so many of our classmates, he and I still live here. Wallace is an only child whose parents own the town's hardware store, a store he'll eventually inherit. When I hear about the pond, I go by the hardware store to find out when he's draining it.

"Saturday morning," Wallace tells me. "You should come see if any of those big bass you claimed to catch back in high school are still in there. At the least you might get back some lures you lost."

"I'll be there," I assure him, though I don't tell him why.

On Saturday I leave at two o'clock when the other shift manager comes in. I no longer live near the pond, but my mother does, so I pull out of the Winn-Dixie where I've worked most of the last twenty years and turn right, pass under Lattimore's one stoplight. On the left are four boarded-up stores, behind them like an anchored cloud the mill's water tower, blue paint chipping off the tank. I drive by Glenn's Café where my ex-wife Angie works, soon after that the small clapboard house where she and our daughter Rose live. The truck belonging to Rose's boyfriend is out front. It's not my week-end to be in charge, as I've been reminded more than once, so I drive on by. At least I know Rose is on the pill. I took her to the clinic myself.

The town ends and there are only farmhouses, most in disrepair—slumping barns and woodsheds, rusty tractors snared by kudzu and trumpet vines. I drive another half-mile and park in front of my mother's house. She comes onto the porch and I know from her expression that she's gotten the week confused and expects to see her granddaughter, is disappointed when only I get out of the car. We talk a few minutes before I tell her I'm going to the pond.

I walk down the sloping land, straddle the sagging barbed wire and make my way through brambles and broom sedge, what once was a pasture. There's a faint indention where the grass was worn away, a path created the summer before my senior year when I'd made this trek three or four evenings a week, lantern and rod in one hand, tackle box in the other. Once school started back, Angie and I would begin dating, and I'd find other things to do in the dark, but this was still summer. I was seventeen and living in a town of three hundred, my days spent bagging groceries. Back then there was no internet, no cable TV or VCRs, at least in our house. Nights I'd listen to the radio or watch TV with my parents, look over college brochures and financial aid forms the guidance counselor had given me. No surprise that the hope of a lunker bass was as exciting as things got around Lattimore.

But it was always more than that. After a day at the grocery store, I wanted to be away from people a while, and the pond at twilight was a good place. Gray cinder blocks bait fisherman used for seats were vacated, but worm containers and tangles of fishing line showed the fishermen had been there. Later in the night, couples would come to the pond. Their leavings were on the bank as well—rubbers and blankets and hair braids, once a pair of panties hung on the white oak's limb. But that hour when day and night made their slow exchange, I had the pond to myself.

Those early evenings I'd untie the jon-boat from the lowest white oak branch free and row out to the pond's center. I would fish until it was neither day nor night, but something in between. Then I'd set my rod and reel down. There never seemed to be a breeze. The water was so smooth that pond and shore were equally still. Nothing seemed to move, as if the world had taken in a soft breath, and was holding it. In those moments, I always imagined that time itself had leveled out, moving neither forward nor back. Then the frogs and crickets waiting for full dark announced themselves. Or a breeze came up and I'd again hear the slosh of water against land, and I'd hear it alone.

Until a Friday evening a few weeks before school started back. I'd gathered my tackle box and rod and lantern, heard again my mother's warning to be careful, and made my way down the pasture and untied the jon-boat from the white oak. Who the boat originally belonged to, I had no idea. Like the pond itself, it had become communal. I had contributed the blue nylon rope, tired of having to swim out to retrieve the boat. I laid my equipment in the bow and pushed away from shore.

The only sound was the swish of the paddle as I rowed to the pond's center. Once there I tied on a Rapala, my favorite lure because I could fish it on the surface or submerged. An afternoon thunderstorm had rinsed the humidity from the air, and the evening was cool, more like early fall. I cast toward the willows on the far bank, where I'd caught bass in the past. After a dozen tries nothing struck, so I paddled closer to the willows and cast into the cove where the creek entered. When I had no luck there I worked the lure around brush piles. A small bass hit and I reeled it in, its red gills flaring as I freed the hook and lowered it back into the water. By then it was almost completely dark, and I was about to light the Coleman lantern when a truck bumped down the dirt road to the pond, its headlights slashing across the water before the vehicle jerked right, halted beside the white oak as the headlights dimmed.

Music came from the truck's open windows and carried over the water with such clarity I recognized the song. The cab light came on and the music stopped. As the minutes passed, stars began stippling the sky, a thick-shouldered moon rimmed up over the ridge. A man and woman got out, the cabin light still on. The jon-boat drifted toward the willows, and I let it. The voices on the far bank rose, became angry. The people were hard to see, more like shadows moving apart and then close. The words softened for a few moments before a sound clear as a rifle shot. The woman fell and the man got back in the cab. The headlights flared and the truck turned around, slinging mud before the tires gained traction. The truck swerved up the dirt road and out of sight.

The woman stood. She moved closer to the bank and sat down on a cinder block. As more stars pierced the sky, and the waxing moon lifted itself over the ridge, I waited for the truck to return, or the woman to walk up the dirt road. But as the minutes passed neither happened. The jon-boat drifted deeper into the willows, their drooping branches raking at my face. I didn't want to move, but the willows had entangled the boat, the graying wood creaking as it bumped against the bank. I pushed away with the paddle. The boat snagged and rocked and the metal tackle box banged against the side.

"Who's out there?" the woman asked, then, as if to further confirm. "I can see you."

I drifted a few more moments, then lit the lantern. I paddled to the pond's center.

"I'm fishing," I said, and lifted the rod and reel, feeling compelled to prove it.

The woman didn't say anything, just continued to sit on the cinderblock. I took a single paddle stroke in her direction and let the boat drift closer to her.

"Are you okay?" I asked.

The woman didn't answer for a few moments.

"My face will be bruised," she finally said. "But no teeth knocked out. No broken nose. Bruises fade. I'll be better off tomorrow than he will."

"Is he coming back?" I asked.

"Yeah, he's coming back. He needs me to drive to Charlotte. Another DUI and he'll be riding around on a bicycle. Anyway, he's just up there."

The woman pointed a quarter mile up the dirt road where a faint square of light hovered like foxfire.

"He's drinking the rest of his whiskey while some hillbilly whines on the radio about how hard life is. When the bottle's empty, he'll be back."

The jon-boat drifted closer to the bank, within a few yards. The woman stood and I dug the paddle's wooden blade into the silt so I kept some distance between us. The lantern's glow fell on both of us now. She was younger than I'd thought, maybe no more than thirty. A large woman, wide-hipped and tall, at least five-eight. Blonde hair that was clearly dyed, a face that might have been pretty if not for the red welt covering the right side. The front of her yellow and blue dress was smeared with mud. She raised her hand and fanned away a haze of insects.

"Are fewer gnats and mosquitoes out there?" she asked. "The damn things are eating me alive."

"Only if I stay near the center," I answered.

I glanced up at the truck.

"I guess I'll get back out there."

I pushed the paddle to turn the bow, deciding to make a few more casts, then beach the boat in the creek cove. I'd work my way through the briars and brush to the pasture and head home.

"Can I get in the boat with you?" the woman asked.

"I'm just going to make a couple of more casts," I answered. "Then I need to get back home."

"Just a few minutes," she said, and gave me a small smile, the hardness in her face and voice lessening. "I'm not going to hurt you. Just a few minutes. To get away from the bugs."

"Can you swim?"

"Yes," she said, and nodded toward the truck. "And he can't. So even if he does come back, just set me on shore and row back out."

The woman brushed some of the dried mud from her skirt, as if to make herself more presentable.

"Just a few minutes."

"Okay," I told her, and moved closer to the bank.

I steadied the jon-boat while she got in the front seat, the lantern at her feet. The woman talked while I paddled, not turning her head, as if addressing the pond.

"I finally get away from this county and that son-of-a-bitch drags me back to visit his sister. She's not home so instead he buys a quart of Wild Turkey and we end up here, with him wanting to lay down on a muddy pond bank with just a horse blanket beneath us. I told him no way, so he gets the jacket out of the truck for me. For my head, he tells me, like that would change my mind. What a prince."

As I lifted the paddle and let the jon-boat drift, she turned to me.

"Nothing like coming back home, right?"

"You're from Lattimore?" I asked.

"No, but this county. Lawndale. You know where that is, don't you?"

"Yes."

"But our buddy in the truck used to live in Lattimore, so we're having a Cleveland County reunion tonight, assuming you aren't just visiting."

"I live here."

"How old are you?" she asked.

"Seventeen."

The woman asked if I was still in high school and when I nodded she smiled.

"We used to kick your asses in football."

I pulled in the paddle when we reached the pond's center. The rod was beside me, but I didn't pick it up.

"When you get back to Charlotte," I asked, "will you call the police?"

"No, they wouldn't do anything. He'll pay though. He had his damn boots and pants off before he saw I wasn't laying down on that blanket with him."

The woman took a billfold from the jacket.

"Left this behind. He got paid yesterday so there's a couple of hundred dollars. I'll take the money and leave the billfold. He'll wake up tomorrow with no money and no driver's license. No jacket, either."

"What if he figures you took it?"

"I can make myself scarce. That's easy to do in Charlotte. Anyway, he'll be back living here soon."

"How do you know that?"

"Women's intuition," she says. "You've heard of that, haven't you? That and the fact that all he talks about is missing this place. He'll move back soon as the mill starts hiring again, and he'll still be here when they pack they pack the dirt over his coffin."

She'd paused and looked at me.

"What about you? Already got a job lined up after high school?"

"I'm going to college."

"College," she said, looking at me closely. "I'd not have thought that. You seem the kind who'd stay around here."

Wallace waves from the opposite bank and makes his way around the pond. His pants and tennis shoes are grimed with mud. Wallace does most of his work indoors, so the July sun has already reddened his face and unsleeved arms. He nods at the valve.

"Damn thing's clogged up twice. Still, it's getting there."

The pond is a red-clay bowl, one-third full. In what was once the shallows, rusty beer cans and Styrofoam bait containers have emerged, two ball caps and a single flip flop. Farther in, Christmas trees and stumps submerged years are now visible, the black branches threaded with red-and-white bobbers and bream hooks, plastic worms and bass plugs, including a six-inch Rapala that I risk the slick mud to pull free. The hooks are so rusty one breaks off.

"Let me see," Wallace says, and examines the lure.

"I used to fish with one like this," I tell him, "the same size and model."

"Probably one of yours then," Wallace says, offers me the lure as if to confirm my ownership. "You want any of these others?"

"No," I answer. "I don't even want that one."

"Well, I'll take them then," Wallace says, lifting a yellow Jitterbug from a limb. "I hear people collect old plugs nowadays. They might be worth a few dollars, add to the hundred I'm getting to do this. The way business has fallen off, I need every dollar I can get."

We move under the big white oak and sit in its shade, watch the pond's slow contraction. More things emerge—a rod and reel, a metal bait bucket, more lures and hooks and bobbers. There are swirls in the water now, fish vainly searching for the upper levels of their world. A large bass leaps near the valve.

Wallace nods at a burlap sack.

"Those bluegill will flush down that drain to the creek, but it looks like some fish will be left to fry up."

We watch the water, soon a steady dimpling on the surface, like rain. Another bass flails upward, shimmers green and silver in the afternoon sun.

"Angie said Rose is trying to get loans so she can go to your alma mater next year," Wallace says.

"It's an alma mater only if you graduate," I reply.

Wallace picks up a stick, scrapes some mud off his shoes. He starts to speak, then hesitates, finally does speak.

"I always admired your taking responsibility like that. Coming back here, I mean, and staying after the divorce. There are many who wouldn't have done that, even back then. Now, hell, nowadays there's women who don't even know or care who their baby's daddy is, much less expect him to marry her. And the men, they're worse. They won't help support a child they brought into the world, don't even want to be a part of its life."

When I don't reply, Wallace checks his watch.

"This is taking longer than I figured," he says. "I'm going to make sure Bobby hasn't closed up early. Then I'm going by the cafe. I haven't had lunch. I can bring you back something."

"A Coke would be nice," I say.

As Wallace drives away, I remember getting out of the jon-boat that night, how when I was about to tie the nylon rope to the white oak branch the woman asked whose boat it was and I told her I didn't know.

"Leave it untied then, I may take it back out again."

"I don't think you should do that," I said. "It might not be safe."

"It depends on what you want to be safe from, doesn't it?" the woman said, fanning at a flurry of gnats that had engulfed us both.

She took a ten-dollar bill out of the billfold.

"Here's something for taking me out on the pond. And this jacket," she said, taking it off. "It's a nice one and he's not getting it back. It looks like a good fit to me."

"I'd better not," I said, and picked up my fishing equipment and the lantern. I paused. "When he comes back, you're not afraid he'll do something else? I mean, I can call the police."

She shook her head.

"Don't do that. Like I said, he needs a driver, so he'll make nice. You go on home now."

And so I did go home, and once there did not call the police or tell my parents. I had trouble sleeping that night, but the next day at work, as the hours passed, I assured myself that if anything really bad had happened, everyone in Lattimore would have known by now.

I went back to the pond, for the last time, that evening. Just to fish, I told myself. The nylon rope was missing but the paddle lay under the front seat. As I got in, I lifted the paddle and found a ten-dollar bill beneath it. I rowed out to the center and tied on the Rapala and threw it at the pond's far bank

As darkness descended, what had seemed certain earlier in the day seemed less so. When a cast landed in some brush, I cranked the reel fast, hoping to avoid snagging the Rapala, but that also caused the lure to go deeper. The rod bowed and I was hung. Any other time, I'd have rowed to the snag and leaned over the gunwale, let my hand follow the line into the water and free the hook. Instead, I tightened the line and gave a hard jerk. The lure stayed where it was.

For a minute I sat there. Something thrashed in the reeds, maybe a muskrat or a bass after a frog. Then the water was still again, not even a breeze's soft ripple. Moonlight brightened, as if the moon itself wished to probe the dark water. I took out my pocketknife, cut the line, and rowed back to shore and beached the boat. That night I dreamed that I'd let my hand follow the line until my fingers were tangled in human hair.

Wallace's truck comes bumping down the dirt road that is now little more than a gully. He hands me my Coke and opens a white bag containing his drink and a hamburger. We sit under the tree.

"It's draining good now," he says.

The fish not inhaled by the drain are more visible, fins sharking the surface. A catfish that easily weighs five pounds wallows onto the bank as if hoping for some sudden evolution. Wallace quickly finishes his hamburger. He takes the burlap sack and walks into what's left of the pond. He hooks a finger through the catfish's gills, drops it into the burlap.

In another half-hour what thinning water remains boils with bass and catfish. More fish beach themselves and Wallace gathers them like fallen fruit, the sack punching and writhing in his grasp.

"You come over tonight," he says to me. "There'll be plenty."

As early evening comes, more stumps and snags emerge, fewer lures. A whiskey bottle and another bait bucket, some cans that probably rolled and drifted into the pond's deep center. Then I see the cinderblock, draped over it what looks like a withered arm. Wallace continues to gather more fish, including a blue cat that will go ten pounds, its whiskers long as nightcrawlers. I walk onto the red slanting mud, move slowly so I won't slip and fall. I stop when I stand only a fishing rod's length from the cinderblock.

"What do you see?" Wallace asks.

I wait for the water to give me an answer, and before long it does. Not an arm but a leather jacket sleeve, tied to the block by a fray of blue nylon. I step into the water and loosen the jacket from the concrete, and as I do I remember the ten dollar bill left in the boat. Her assumption that I'd be the one to find it.

I feel something in the jacket's right pocket and pull out a withered billfold. Inside are two silted shreds of thin plastic, a driver's license, some other card now indiscernible. No bills.

I stand in the pond's center and toss the billfold's remnants into the drain. I drop the jacket and step back as Wallace gills a foot-long bass, the last fish that hasn't escaped down the drain. Wallace knots the sack and lifts it, the veins in his bicep and forearm taut as he does so.

"That's at least fifty pounds of fish," he says, and sets the sack back down. "Let me clear this drain one more time. Then I'm going home to cook these up."

Wallace leans over the drain and claws away the clumps of mud and wood. The remaining water gurgles down the pipe.

"I hate to see this old pond go," he says. "I guess the older you get the less you like any kind of change."

Wallace lifts the sack of fish and pulls it over his shoulder. We walk out of the pond as dusk comes on. By the time Wallace struggles onto the bank he has to pause to catch his breath.

"You going to come over later," he asks.

"Not tonight."

"Another time then," Wallace says.

After Wallace drives off, I sit on the bank a few minutes. Shadows deepen where the water was, making it appear that the pond has refilled. By the time I'm over the barbed wire fence, I can look back and I can no longer tell what was and what is.

READING THE PAPER

Sharon Olds

When I'm looking at the women in headscarves, walking through
their city, to protest marital rape
and the law that women can't learn to read,
and I start to write about the crowd of men
howling against them — it looks as if they want
to tear a woman apart, and maybe
have at her, first, while the torso still has
a head and a limb, the minimum
to make it consensual — I notice
that as I write I am feeling something
positive, I am liking being
out on the water of words, at the oar
of the craft of a sentence. It was the earliest
form of fair government
I knew, the sentence — each part of it
played well with others — subject, verb,
object, the object never got up out of the
sentence, and went over and hit
the subject. What I want for everyone
is to have a pencil, a piece of paper.
What I want for girls is an alphabet,
left to right, or right to left — let's
do one line from right to left:
                    ,D ,C ,B ,A
what does a woman want — eyes
to read, a tongue, every part
of speech — the AB, AB of a beating heart.

90

A WHOLE NEW LIFE

(an excerpt)

Reynolds Price

So by daylight on July 3rd, morning thoughts of a stiff sobriety were plainly in order. But in the midst of such circular thinking an actual happening intervened with no trace of warning. I was suddenly not propped in my brass bed or even contained in my familiar house. By the dim new, thoroughly credible light that rose around me, it was barely dawn; and I was lying fully dressed in modern street clothes on a slope by a lake I knew at once. It was the big lake of Kinnereth, the Sea of Galilee, in the north of Israel—green Galilee, the scene of Jesus' first teaching and healing.

Still sleeping around me on the misty ground were a number of men in the tunics and cloaks of first-century Palestine. I soon understood with no sense of surprise that the men were Jesus' twelve disciples and that he was nearby asleep among them. So I lay on a while in the early chill, looking west across the lake to Tiberias, a small low town, and north to the fishing villages of Capernaum and Bethsaida.

Then one of the sleeping men woke and stood.

I saw it as Jesus, bound toward me. He looked much like the lean Jesus of Flemish paintings—tall with dark hair, unblemished skin and a self-possession both natural and imposing.

Again I felt no shock or fear. All this was normal human event; it was utterly clear to my normal eyes and was happening as surely as any event of my previous life. I lay and watched him walk on nearer.

Jesus bent and silently beckoned me to follow. I knew to shuck off my trousers and jacket, then my shirt and shorts. Bare, I followed him.

He was wearing a twisted white cloth round his loins; otherwise he was bare and the color of ivory. We waded out into cool lake water twenty feet from shore till we stood waist-deep.

I was in my body but was also watching my body from slightly upward and behind. I could see the purple dye on my back, the long rectangle that boxed my thriving tumor.

Jesus silently took up handfuls of water and poured them over my head and back till water ran down my puckered scar. Then he spoke once— "Your sins are forgiven"—and turned to shore again, done with me.

I came on behind him, thinking in standard greedy fashion, *It's not my sins I'm worried about.* So to Jesus' receding back I had the gall to say "Am I also cured?"

He turned to face me, no sign of a smile, and finally said two words— "That too." Then he climbed from the water, not looking round, really done with me.

I followed him out and then, with no palpable seam in the texture of time or place, I was home again in my wide bed.

Was it a dream I gave myself in the midst of a catnap, thinking I was awake? Was it a vision of the sort accorded from a maybe external source to mystics of differing degrees of sanity through human history? From the moment my mind was back in my own room, no more than seconds after I'd left it, I've believed that the event was an external gift, however brief, of an alternate time and space in which to live through a crucial act.

For me the clearest support for that conclusion survives on paper in my handwriting. I've mentioned the sparseness of my calendar notes—hard happenings only, not thoughts or speculations. And in my calendar for '84, at the top of the space for Tuesday, July 3rd, I've drawn a small star and written

6 a.m.—By Kinnereth, the bath, "Your sins are forgiven"—"Am I cured?"—"That too."

BLACK OLIVES

Michael Waters

In those days while my then-wife

taught English to a mustached young nurse who hoped to join

her uncle's practice in Queens,

I'd sip gin on our balcony and listen to her

read aloud from the phrasebook,

then hear the student mimic, slowly, *Where does it hurt?*

then my wife repeat those words

so the woman might enunciate each syllable,

until I could no longer

bear it, so I'd prowl the Ambelokipi district

attempting to decipher

titles emblazoned on marquees—*My Life As A Dog,*

Runaway Train, Raging Bull—

then stroll past dark shops that still sold only one item—

kerosene, soap, cheese, notebooks—

to step down into the shop that sold olives, only

olives in barrels riddling

a labyrinth of dank aisles and buttressing brick walls.

I'd sidle among squat drums,

fingering the fruit, thumbing their inky shine, their rucked

skins like blistered fingertips,

their plump flesh, the rough salts needling them, judging their cowled

heft, biding my time. Always

I'd select a half-kilo of the most misshapen,

sprung from the sacred rubble below Mt. Athos, then
had to shout "Fuck Kissinger!"
three times before the proprietor would allow me
to make my purchase, then step
back out into the smut-stirred Athens night to begin
the slow stroll home, bearing now
my little sack of woe, oil seeping through brown paper,
each olive brought toward my mouth
mirroring lights flung from marquees and speeding taxis,
each olive burning its coal–
flame of bitterness and history into my tongue.
wrinkled and blackest olives

Michael Water's office

THEATRICS
Mark Powell

At some point you had to get out. You had to get out, she thought, or it killed you. But that wasn't true. That was what Roosevelt would have referred to as one of her theatrical responses, her failure to exist beyond the performative, the reenactment of old wrongs, the slings and arrows and all-around bad shit laid on her by her nana. In truth, it wasn't so much that you were killed as warped, you bent in a series of compromises, each uglier than the one before. Though it wasn't so much your malleability that was at issue as the slow wasting of—and here she caught herself on the edge of theatrics—the slow wasting of your very soul. But this man—this white man—Luther Lyle was no more interested in such than Rose had been.

"You think I don't hear that drug shit twenty-four seven?" Lyle asked. He stood behind the display case and leaned toward her, hands planted on the glass. "You think I don't get tired of watching y'all come in here wanting and wanting what you can't get?"

But Jordan just wanted her knife, Roosevelt's knife, and she didn't see it beside the pocket watches and repackaged copies of *Call of Duty* and *Grand Theft Auto*. She had the fifty dollars to get it out of hock now, but if it was gone, if it was gone she didn't know what would happen. She was coming off a bad jag—she had been dreaming of the bear again—and had a single Xanax left, but if Rose's knife was gone it wouldn't help. She'd spiral and she didn't want to spiral, Jesus, not again.

She smoothed two twenties and a crumpled ten.

"I just want my knife back."

"That knife's a piece of work," Lyle said. "It's crossed my mind a time or two to just hang onto it."

"You said you'd keep it for me."

"I did. But the thing with all you dope heads." He scratched one gray temple sighed and turned to unlock a cabinet behind him. "Y'all ain't the most reliable demographic." When he turned back around he had the knife in his hand but didn't yet pass it over. "This is a W.E. Pease," he said. "Look here. That's a Mortise handle. Every bit of it ivory. These are mosaic studs all along here."

"Just give it to me."

"This is a six, seven hundred dollar knife. I did you a serious favor hanging onto this thing."

He slapped it into her hand and she pushed the money at him.

"Keep it," he said. "He came in and paid it off already."

She stared at him a moment. He was talking about Leighton.

"He said you'd run off," Lyle said. "But I guess you didn't run far enough."

She put the knife in her pocket and left, walked the length of the block. She felt the pang of losing him again, Rose. They had fought, of course, fought because the Florida nights were stifling; fought because breathing was like pulling rags from your lungs, fought because everybody fought, given enough time. Fought because somewhere in this world—God only knew where—was a child whose name Jordan refused to speak. She had decided to forgive Rose, but standing outside The Olympian Billiards & Cocktail Lounge she was undecided. He had cost Jordan her child, cost Jordan her life. But no use thinking about it now, not now or ever again.

She pushed open the door. It was almost six and the place was beginning to fill with folks shooting pool or drinking at tables, twenty-somethings in expensive hiking gear. The older grimmer crowd sat at the bar and stared silently at a pay-per-view fight. From the back she heard the animated swoosh of the Golden Tee video game.

She took a barstool and ordered a glass of Chardonnay. She wanted to do things right. That was all she had ever wanted. Right glass. Right wine. Everything in its ordered place. A man sat and smiled in her direction before he turned to the bartender. Good looking in a blue sport coat, his face a construction of right-angles, his hair neat and flecked with gray. They were forever following her, older men, and she was forever indulging them, first Rose and then Leighton, dying on the rack of adulation. He moved to the stool beside her, bourbon in one hand, wine in the other.

"I took the liberty," he said, handing her the glass.

"What a gentlemen."

He smiled and she started to drink then remembered the knife and dropped one hand into her lap to touch it through the denim of her jeans.

The man pointed at the drink. "Clos du Bois. I didn't misjudge?"

"Oh, no," she said. "A gentleman with a good eye."

"Or ear. I'm Tom."

"Jordan."

"That's a lovely name."

She batted her eyes wildly. "You can't imagine how often I hear that."

He gave back a sheepish grin. He really was good looking.

"I'm joking," she said, and left a little smear of lipstick on the rim like a gift. "So you're local, Tom?"

"Semi," he said. "I've got a practice in Atlanta that I'm gradually stepping away from. Got a place in the mountains now."

"You're a lawyer?"

"Reconstructive surgeon."

"Is that like a plastic surgeon?"

"Plastic surgeon. Sure, why not." He laughed. "You're something, aren't you? I'd like to fire you out of a cannon."

They moved to a table and Jordan drank a third glass while Tom rattled on about his time-share in Barbados. She had lost the thread of the conversation and was no longer listening, no longer even looking at him but over his shoulder and around the room. The stereo wailed drunken country love and around them couples started to pair off, hesitantly, almost tenderly, she thought, not yet drunk enough to have forgotten what it means to be lonely. But when she looked out the front window she thought she saw Leighton's Navigator idling along the street but that was the paranoia is all that was. Put it out of your mind, Jordan. Don't let it creep in.

She raised the glass so that it caught the overhead light.

Don't let it. Don't you dare.

But it had and she ran from the table and cut the line to the ladies room where she palmed water to swallow her last Xanax. A woman in a Mossy Oak camouflage ball cap and a black tank-top looked at her in the mirror and asked if she was all right.

"Yeah," Jordan said. She was sweating but she was going to be all right. She was sweating but everybody sweated. It meant you were still alive. "Just saw somebody."

"Well, kill his ass, sister." The woman lit a cigarette. "They ain't a one of em worth the dick swinging between their legs."

"I have to go home," Jordan told her reflection.

"Don't let him run you."

"I just need to go home."

"Well go home, but don't let him run you."

When she walked back to the bar she didn't bother looking toward the street. It was dark now, and the window was a glossy mirror, a frame for sensible people laughing and drinking. She didn't need to hide. Tom was gone and she didn't need to hide. She had ways of disappearing in plain sight. You threw yourself against a wall and whatever stuck they accepted; meanwhile the self slunk away, undetected. You didn't bother with any disguise. That was the secret: you didn't bother with anything.

She ordered a gin and tonic and when the bartender brought it she handed him one of the twenties. He was middle-aged and homely, a second-generation barkeep who appeared to have resigned himself to much less.

"I'd take that money and put it down on a bus ticket," he said. He looked out at the street and bent closer. "He was in here earlier looking for you."

When she asked who he simply shook his head and walked away. She knew who, but this was theatrics, her performative state. She couldn't help it. She finished her drink and left.

She was two blocks up the street when she noticed the lights behind her and instead of playing coy she simply turned and walked toward them, watched the window slide down on Leighton Clatter. He had pulled into one of the angled spaces and she could feel the warm air radiate from the floor vents.

"I thought you might need a ride," he said.

"I'm walking."

"It's late to be walking."

"It's not that late."

He let his hand drift out toward her so that she saw the rings bunched on his fat fingers. "You're too pretty to be out alone."

"It's an affliction."

"Hilarious. You know you really should worry more."

"I'm fine."

She felt him stiffen and could sense the change in his voice even before he spoke: "Get in the car, Jordan."

He backed out and they eased up the street past Blue Ridge Medical supply with its shower stools and electric scooters, Rexall Drugs, the Gun Shoppe, the offices of the Department of Social Services housed down in the old fire station. They were building a new courthouse, four floors of courtrooms and, she guessed, holding rooms. The money was coming from property taxes levied on the new developments dotting the mountains that ringed town. The money was coming from people like Leighton.

After Rose, she had come home and got her old job at the fish camp back, rented a dump on Short Street, spent her tips on rhinestones and cocaine. The night she met Leighton she was all lower vibration, strung out and in desperate need, and then someone told her Leighton was holding, and that was how she wound up having sex with him atop a cardboard box marked LIGHT BULBS—FRAGILE!!. He was a disgusting man but she felt reckless, one remove from the worst desperation she'd ever felt. So in an attic room of wall studs and sheets of silver and pink insulation Jordan slid into his lap and kissed him while he slipped down the strap of her bra and licked around her dark nipples, heels grinding the floorboards as he swam into her.

She had spiraled after that, a down-racing arc that ended only when she was Baker-Acted in the fall. Her nana's work: three days in two-point restraints at Saint Francis in Greenville. After that were the attempts at normalcy, the friends who would take her home and try to teach her to how to live. Bridal showers and barbecues. Trips to the mall in Greenville. There were girls' nights out that ended with Jordan unconscious or weeping then there were no more nights out and then there were no more girls. She didn't miss it. *Sentimentality,* she remembered from the Jung she had read at the spiritualist camp, *is the superstructure erected upon brutality.* She didn't miss it one bit. She had simply called Leighton. She hadn't seen him for almost a year, but soon enough she was a kept woman, waking beneath the spidery blades of his ceiling fan, lying on his four-poster bed like a gutted fish. Later, he paid for her to get clean, but then she never really got clean. She just went back to her grandparents.

"I've missed you," he said. "Got worried for a bit."

"Well you shouldn't have."

"Heard a nasty rumor that someone saw you all the way up in Asheville hanging around with the local shit." He kept his eyes forward. "I got so worried I almost went over and saw Littlejon, thought to ask him what had become of his granddaughter."

She said nothing, and he clicked the blinker to turn onto Short Street by the abandoned car wash. Someone had left a couch on the sidewalk and it was covered with garbage bags.

"I missed you, Jordan."

"You said that already."

He looked at her. "You're in one of your moods tonight. All right. I can accept that." He pulled to a stop outside the house she was renting. "But don't go slumming on me, and don't make me worry again, you understand me?"

She reached for the door and he grabbed her arm, switched his hand to her cheeks so fast she gasped, the meat of his fingers wringing her mouth so that it puckered like a child's.

"I'm refusing to take the long view. You understand me?" He dug his rings into her skin. "You don't run out on me."

"All right," she managed to say.

"My patience is vast, but it's not infinite. Not at my age."

"All right."

"Good. But before you go I'd like an apology. Say you're sorry, Jordan."

"I'm sorry."

"Say you're sorry for making Leighton worry. Say you're sorry for breaking old Leighton's heart."

Her mouth was beginning to hurt. "Please," she said. "I'm sorry."

He nodded her head up and down slowly.

"I'll see you this weekend."

When he pushed her toward the door she almost fell out and then did, scrambling up as he peeled past the stop sign and out of sight. She straightened her coat and touched her front pocket; the knife was still there; she still had the knife, and thought of Rose and his Pilgrim angel, Rose dying on a rented hospital bed in Florida. For whatever else he was, he was hers.

Or had been. But she had been so young, so young and so stupid. And what could she have possibly known, naïve as she was? She knew now you could love someone on the strength of being young. You could love someone on the strength of wide hands that touch softly, that certain smell that lingers along the back of the neck. You could love someone because you are poor together, misunderstood together, lonely and cast to your own inadequate devices together. You sleep late and make love on white sheets. Touch constantly. Smell like laundry and taste like cotton candy.

Those days driving south when they would stay in bed until noon and then rise, bodies humid and feral with sex. You could love someone on the strength of all that, before the reckoning, before the petals wilt and then fall, first singly, then a mad shower that tastes like nothing so much as what is lost.

You could love someone on that, but not forever.

She unlocked the front door and walked through the kitchen and then room to room. No one was home. Her cousin Willis had moved in right after he'd lost his job at Duke Power and with him had come a steady parade of his friends about whom the best thing she could say was that they tended to be temporary, coming and going so quickly she never bothered with names. The door to Willis's bedroom was cracked and she edged it open until it caught on the extension cord that ran to the empty fish tank, its dry seafloor cluttered with rocks and a busted pump.

The room was a mess—patches of drywall flaked onto the carpet beneath a sagging Bob Marley flag—and looking at it made her almost physically sick. She flicked off the bedroom light and watched the glow-in-the-dark stars flex on the ceiling. The room was a mess, the entire house was a mess, and what she was doing was living in filth. Her nana's expression. She was living in filth. Living in sin. But that was alright. She was here.

She was still alive.

104

The cat is Fitz, and he is a demon from hell. I have a second, shyer one named Durkan, and one or the other is sure to be upon me the minute I sit down to write. Fitz was born without a tail, and Durkan -- grey and white -- has an exceptionally long one. (Fitz is a big ripper and chewer of cardboard.)
-- Nathalie Anderson

DE PROFUNDIS

Nathalie F. Anderson

MEMORIAL WINDOWS

ST. MARY'S, SWAFFHAM PRIOR, CAMBRIDGESHIRE

Whatever would possess a congregation to glass its nave
with armament? Small church, small village, poised at the verge
of the fens, farmers and their sons, dons and dons' daughters –
nothing particularly military round about it. Yet here
at boy's eye height stands a bright boy bugler (wake up
the mighty men), and here are women trim as Gibson girls,
those prim long-skirted tennis players, advantageously employed
at packing shells. One window's dedicated to the works of war –

a signal tent, a captured trench (though they dig into hell) –
and one is dedicated to war's mitigation – chaplain,
water in the desert, Red Cross van – but both lights rise at last
to weaponry: a howitzer (*the blast is as a storm
against the wall*); rays of liquid fire; a sub and a sub-marine
strewer of mines (*thence will I command the serpent
and he shall bite*); a tin tank, riveted, peculiarly
bobbined (*the man that shall touch them must be fenced in iron*).

Vidimus, medieval glaziers called the sketch stretched out
for the King's approval, a full-sized whitened table or
sturdy pieced-together tablet where the shaped glass
would be laid down, color matched to color, for the joining.
Here is a zeppelin, bone-white by moonlight, convoyed by stars.
Here is the Lusitania, sinking. The terror by night, *vidimus*;
the vapour of smoke, *vidimus*; beneath great waters, among
false brethren – *vidimus, vidimus*: we have seen it.

And here a bi-plane breasts the storm, a picture so appealing
the church sells postcards of it. The clouds it flies are Prussian blue
blustering towards bruise, no angels anywhere in sight. Against that stark
and squalling dark, its snub nose, banty wheels, and paper wings
show bold: wan but willing, spunky, all its struts and pipings
picked out in palest gold. A French-built SPAD, flown by British pilots
and Americans, though here – half-obscured by a cross-bar – the iron cross
brands it as German. *"Though they climb up to heaven,"* reads the scripture

chosen for it, *"thence will I bring them down"* – though "safely down"
or "ruthlessly," each one who prays here must decide. *All ye works
of the Lord, Bless ye the Lord*: St. Mary's windows book-end the war,
1914 to 1919, Benediction to Memorial, exuberance to devastation.
There's a third window, too, devoted to peace: springtime and harvest,
green glass and gold glass, the shepherding of sheep. No one talks about it.
Progress, progress, civilization: outside the village, poppies
bleeding through the corn. *Blessed are the dead which die in the Lord.*

THE POWER OF LOVE: A MEDITATION ON SOUTH AFRICA
Anthony S. Abbott

"It is my own belief that the only power which can resist the power of fear is the power of love. It's a weak thing and a tender thing: men despise and deride it. But I look for the day when in South Africa we shall realize that the only lasting and worth-while solution of our grave and profound problems lies not in the use of power, but in that understanding and compassion without which human life is an intolerable bondage, condemning us all to an existence of violence, misery and fear."

—Alan Paton

"There is a lovely road that runs from Ixopo into the hills. These hills are grass-covered and rolling, and they are lovely beyond any singing of it."   I cannot keep the tears from my eyes as I read these words, these astonishingly beautiful words that form the opening sentences of Alan Paton's novel, *Cry, The Beloved Country,* which was published in 1948, the year in which the Nationalist party won South Africa's elections and established the apartheid government which lasted until 1994, when Nelson Mandela was elected President.

I do not know when I first read *Cry, The Beloved Country.* I know that John Patterson, the headmaster of Kent School in Connecticut, from which I graduated in 1953, was a huge admirer of Paton and that Paton was one of the people invited to participate in Kent's celebration of its 50th anniversary in 1956. So I must have read it by then. When I took my graduate oral exams in English at Harvard University, I was asked by one of my examiners to name my two favorite 20th Century British authors. I said, "Joseph Conrad and Alan Paton." "Who?" he asked. He had never heard of Alan Paton. In those days, one didn't read South African or Australian or Canadian writers. He was not impressed with my answer. But the fact remains that *Cry, The Beloved Country* was, quite possibly, my favorite novel. It is a novel of unsurpassed beauty whose prose has the rhythms of the King James Bible and the lyricism of Gerard Manley Hopkins. It is also a novel that tells us if we do not love one another, we will destroy ourselves. "I have one great fear in my heart," says the young black priest, Msimangu, "that one day when they turn to loving they will find we are turned to hating."

I carried the memory of these words, of this novel, through the struggles of the '60's, and as I read James Baldwin and Malcolm X, I understood more and more fully what Msimangu meant. In South Africa the Sharpeville Massacre in 1960 turned Black African leaders toward violence, and led to the imprisonment of Nelson Mandela and other leaders of both the African National Congress (ANC) and the more radical Pan African Congress (PAC). Alan Paton, upon his return from New York, had his passport revoked, and was never, after that allowed out of the country.

I don't remember what I knew then or what I thought then about all this. Paton drifted out of my consciousness. I was raising a family, I was teaching English at Davidson College and thinking about Martin Luther King and Bobby Kennedy and the war in Vietnam. I directed a play by the Jesuit priest Daniel Berrigan called *The Trial of the Catonsville Nine.* I marched with students to the Post Office to deliver letters to President Nixon while the secretaries at the college stood in their windows and waved American flags. For a long time I did not think of South Africa. Alan Paton died of throat cancer in 1988. I must have known that, but I do not remember it.

Nor do I remember what I thought when Mandela and de Klerk were awarded the Nobel Peace prize in 1993 or what I felt when he was inaugurated as president of South Africa on May 10, 1994. Then came, in 2009, the film *Invictus.* I did not know the story of Mandela's extraordinary efforts in

1995 to use the Rugby World Cup as a way of bring South African whites and blacks together in their support for the Springboks, the African National Team. When I saw the scene early in the film where Mandela told the white employees in his office that he wanted them to stay on in their jobs and work next to the blacks, I was astounded and touched. I saw the movie several times, and paid close attention to Mandela's words. He was a prophet. And then it came to pass, purely by accident, but surely as an unexpected gift, that my wife, Susan, and I could travel to South Africa and spend eight days in Capetown and at an animal reserve northwest of Pretoria. We were to leave home on October 30, 2010 and return on November 10.

In preparation for the trip my wife and I began to read. A former student of mine, Jacquie Bussie, now a Professor of Religion at Capital University in Columbus, Ohio, had taken a group of students to South Africa to study racial issues and living conditions. That trip was a life-changing one for her and her students. Read Desmond Tutu's book, *No Future Without Forgiveness*, she said. It is the most important book we read. Tutu, himself a winner of the Nobel Peace Prize, had been made the head of the Truth and Reconciliation Commission formed after Mandela was elected President. It was the Commission's job to investigate the crimes committed under apartheid—not just white crimes but black crimes, too—and they reached the conclusion that truth was more important than punishment, that reconciliation was more important than revenge. There could be no moving forward in South Africa until the truth had been told, and as readers of this wonderful and painful book, we share the truth as it is unfolded to the commission by victims and perpetrators alike. After confession comes forgiveness. With forgiveness ancient enemies can begin to work as friends. This is the blessed truth that South Africa can teach us, and everywhere we went on our trip, we saw blacks, and coloureds (those of mixed race) and whites working together, traveling together, eating and drinking and playing together. Yes, there was poverty, terrible poverty, and lingering remnants of the apartheid regime, which I will come back to shortly, but there was a huge step forward, a huge reason for hope in this beautiful land.

Our second "Bible" was the 600 page biography of Nelson Mandela, by Martin Meredith. Mandela was born on the 18th of July, 1918, and what this means to the student of his life is that you must learn the history of South Africa in the twentieth century in order to understand Mandela and understand Mandela's life in order to make sense of the history. Going to South Africa without this knowledge is a little bit like going to Rome or Florence with no knowledge of Michelangelo or Bernini. I am so glad we did this reading, because it made the people and the history and the land-scape of this beautiful country more real to us, more immediate.

I remember arriving in Cape Town after dark on Sunday, October 31. We had been traveling for two days, and the fourteen members of our group had just been ushered into our bus by our guide, Deon. We had no sooner left the airport than we saw on either side of the highway literally thousands of shacks, most of them made of corrugated metal. After the election of Mandela in 1994, virtually millions of people were on the move. Blacks came from all over South Africa into Johannesburg and Cape Town, looking for jobs, and they lived in these shacks. Mandela swore as President that his government would build houses for all these people, and they worked very hard at it. Later in our visit, we travelled to two of the townships, just outside of Cape Town, where most of these people lived, and we could see both the progress and the impossible task of fulfilling the needs of these people. In the largest of these townships, Khayelitsa, with a population of 1.2 million, we visited Vicky's B and B (see www.vickysbandb.com) and listened to her talk about the daunting task of educating the children, finding jobs, cleaning up the streets, fighting AIDS and other diseases. Vicky collects pens, pencils, and notebooks for the students in the school, who have no money at all for any school supplies, and she uses her website to reach people all over the world.

At the end of our trip, on our final day, we visited Soweto and heard a talk from Thulani Madondo, the head of the Kliptown Youth Program. His situation is even more desperate than Vicky's. Most of the inhabitants of Kliptown, one of the very oldest sections of Soweto, founded in 1903, have no electricity, no running water, no sanitation, no access to health clinics. Unemployment is over 70%. His program supplies tutoring, athletic programs and arts programs for the youth of Kliptown, who would otherwise be part of gang life on the streets.

Certainly, I can confess at the outset that I had never heard of Khayelitsa, nor had I heard of Kliptown, even though it was the place the Freedom Charter was signed in 1955. Soweto I knew, because of the Soweto Riots of 1976, but the fact that visits to these townships were included in our tour is of extraordinary significance. In Khayelitsa, in addition to Vicky, we met potters and painters and weavers . In Soweto we visited the home of Nelson Mandela at 8115 Vilakazi Street, the home he lived in from 1946 until his arrest in 1964. We saw the bullet holes in the walls where shots were fired, and heard the words of ordinary people from the neighborhood who knew him and both his first wife, Evelyn, and his second wife, Winnie—the house he lived in for only eleven days after his release from prison in 1990, because his life with Winnie had deteriorated so terribly.

And, of course, we went to Robben Island, next to the Cape of Good Hope itself, the best known site in all of South Africa. No one goes to Cape Town without going to Robben Island unless the wind roughs the waters up and the ferries stop running. We were lucky. We had a nice day, and we as our guide Yasien Mohamed, who takes only special groups around the island. We were special, because our group included the Palestinian Ambassador to Jordan and his party. Though he was not a prisoner at Robben island himself, Yasien knew most of the political prisoners because he had been a behind-the-scenes worker for the cause of freedom. Whenever Mandela came back to Robben island after 1994, Yasien was his guide. He also guided Hilary Clinton around the island (not Bill, he was too busy in Washington).

Yasiem is a remarkable man—funny, thoughtful, deeply concerned for the welfare of his people. "In England they have watches, in Africa we have time," he said. Or, about the fact that the eucalyptus trees, brought in from Australia, were using up the entire water supply of the island: "the eucalyptus is very much like Australians themselves. It has a drinking problem." He took us all over the island and stopped at the lime quarry where all the political prisoners were forced to work, without sunglasses, until the sun and the lime dust severely damaged their eyes. To this day, photographers are not allowed to use flash when they photograph Mandela, because of the damage done to his eyes. "You are standing on the campus of a university—the University of the Limestone Quarry," Yasiem told us, because it was here that the prisoners shared what they were learning not only with one another but with the guards. And some of those guards became Mandela's friends and served as his honor guard at his inauguration.

Yasiem showed us the houses that were used when Robben Island was a leper colony, we saw the World War II cannon that was delivered to the island two years after the war was over. The most moving thing we saw was the isolation unit where Robert Sobukwe, the leader of the Pan African Congress, was kept in solitary confinement for so long that he lost the use of his vocal chords. Sobukwe, Yasiem told us, was considered even more important and dangerous than Mandela. We ended our visit by going into the prison itself and walking into the courtyard where Mandela buried the pages of his famous autobiography, *The Long March to Freedom*, and we passed by his cell, where every morning he completed a rigorous exercise program to keep himself fit, and where he repeated to himself the words of his favorite poem, "Invictus":

Out of the night that covers me,
Black as the Pit from pole to pole,
I thank whatever gods may be
For my unconquerable soul.

In the fell clutch of circumstance
I have not winced nor cried aloud.
Under the bludgeonings of chance
My head is bloody, but unbowed.

Beyond this place of wrath and tears
Looms but the Horror of the shade,
And yet the menace of the years
Finds, and shall find, me unafraid.

It matters not how strait the gate
How charged with punishments the scroll,
I am the master of my fate,
I am the captain of my soul.

Later in our trip, at the request of one of our group, I recited the poem to the whole group as our bus was approaching Soweto. And I will never think of that poem in the same way again. I will always associate it now both with Nelson Mandela and with that cell on Robben Island where he suffered and prepared himself for the task ahead of him.

We left Robben Island and took the ferry back to Cape Town, where we boarded our bus and went to lunch at the Five Flies, one of the most beautiful restaurants in Cape Town. The contrast was both stunning and ironic. Here we were eating lamb and drinking lovely South African wine, and it occurs to me now that contrast was really the theme of our trip. On the day that we visited the townships and went to Vicky's B and B, we drove afterwards to the Kirstenbosch Gardens, one of the four or five most impressive botanical gardens in the world. Here we saw a whole range of Protea, including the majestic King Proteus, and we saw the Bird of Paradise and a tiny little black, blue-throated bird that looked like a hummingbird. We saw the whole garden set against the blue sky and the back of Table Mountain and the Lion's head.

The most vivid and memorable sights we saw were the animals. There can be no more striking contrast than Pilanseberg National Park where we spent three days and the massive slums of Soweto we drove to directly from the park. At the park we saw elephants in herds, and giraffes nibbling nobly from the tops of trees, we saw zebras and hippos and rhinos. We saw three of the Big Five. We saw antelope, and wildebeest and impala, we saw the springbok, South Africa's national animal. And most memorably, twice, we saw an elephant in the road and had to ride behind it until we found a safe turn out, because you cannot pass an elephant on the road. I like that. The road belongs to the elephants. It is their park, and we are privileged to be guests in their world. They remind us that time is something we invented. The elephant is walking down the road, and we must wait. Isn't that lovely? We must stop and remember that we, too, are animals, and that we must respect the dignity of that slow, easy, lumbering walk down the road.

On our last day our tour leader asked us what our favorite event was, and there were many answers. Some said the Cape of Good Hope itself, the huge waves smashing against the rocks where the Atlantic meets the Indian Ocean. Most said, Robben Island, partly because of Yasien and partly, of course, because of Mandela. I said, "Elephant Interaction."

On one of the days we stayed in Pilanesberg, six of us took the opportunity to go visit some elephants at close range. There were six of them, five adults and a baby, and they were brought in from the veld to stand for us at the foot of a stone wall, over which they could extend their heads and trunks. We took handfuls of food from buckets and we fed the elephants. We touched their rough skin, and we said, "Trunk Up," and they raised their trunks and opened their mouths, and we set the food gently on their soft, smooth, pink tongues. It was extraordinary. We felt privileged to be close to these wise, old gentle creatures. We fed them again and again, and called them by name, and the baby, who was not supposed to be fed, put his front feet over the stone wall and begged to be touched, to be fed, to be played with. I had not expected this. It caught me by surprise and made me realize I would never have done anything like this if I had not been given this chance. Now, weeks later, I still feel that soft tongue on my finger tips.

Contrasts. Earlier in the week we had gone to the wine country, and we all had a splendid tour of "La Petite Ferme," in Franschhoek, not far from the better known town of Paarl. The setting was exquisite, as we ate and drank on a lovely stone terrace overlooking rolling hills and vineyards that could have been Italy or Napa Valley. We were totally at peace, and virtually the entire group voted this their best meal. After lunch we drove to Victor Verster Prison, just outside Paarl, where Mandela was held for the last two years of his imprisonment, and from which he was released on February 11, 1990. Outside the gate is a statue of Mandela, his right arm raised in triumph. We stopped there to pay tribute.

What else is there to say? When I got home, people kept asking me if I had a nice time? No, I wanted to say. Sweet Jesus, what use is nice? I am seventy-five years old, and nice is not enough. I was moved by this trip, stirred by this trip, changed in some fundamental way by this trip. "Nice" is hardly the word. There remains an indelible image of the people of South Africa— the potters and the painters and the sculptors in the townships making art out of their lives. Our astonishing guide, Deon, who always wanted to teach us something new, who kept giving us words—especially the word "ubuntu," which means "humanity." or, as many South Africans themselves say, "I am a person through other persons." The highest compliment you can give a person is to say that he or she has or is "ubuntu." I marvel at what the South African people have achieved by bringing together black and white and Indian and Asian in such a remarkable way. I marvel at the cheerfulness of these people, and their refusal to be defeated in the face of staggering poverty and unemployment. I marvel at the beauty of this land—the mix of the animals, the landscape, and the human beings, this beloved country that Alan Paton loved so much and that Nelson Mandela lived to restore to its proper dignity. It is "lovely beyond any singing of it."

THE GREATEST

Robert Hedin

What I remember most about Muhammad Ali
Are not the fast hands and loose, graceful footwork.
Or Manila or Zaire. Or even what came after—
The slurred speech, the sad slow shuffle.
No, what I remember is a boy somewhere
In the foothills of the snowy Zagros Mountains,
A small Kurdish boy in a long blue robe
Who gave us directions that day we were lost,
And how he knew nothing of America
But two syllables he sang over and over
In the high unbroken voice of a girl—
Ali, Ali—then laughed and all at once
Began to bob and weave, jabbing and juking,
His robe flaring a moment like a fighter's.
Ali. One word, two bright syllables
That turned to smoke in the morning air.
And he pointed down the long, dusty road
To Hatra and Ur, the ruins of Babylon,
And the two ancient rivers we had read about,
Their dark starless waters draining away into fog.

PART THREE

LIBERATION

Abigail DeWitt

Had there been sirens during the night? Often she dreamed of sirens when there were none, slept through them when they were right at the edge of town. At first, every wail, every explosion, no matter how distant, sent them racing to the cellar. Maman, Papa, Jeanine and she crouched near the wine crates, and her heart beat in her ears. But after awhile, they gave up going downstairs. She and Jeanine climbed into Maman's bed, burrowing into her rich sleep smell; their father stood in the doorway, as if he could hold off the bombs with his bare hands. Then even that was too much trouble; there was only so much fear a body could hold. Now, if she heard anything during the night, she pulled her pillow over her head.

The hunger was worse, the craving for sweets, for a juicy steak, a loaf of bread, butter in the potatoes and hot chocolate for breakfast, pork loin and marmalade and butter; more than anything she wanted butter—still, it seemed to her that there had been sirens during the night, but who could say?

She didn't always hear things the way the others did. The confusion never lasted long—a few minutes maybe—but there were times when a mosquito sounded louder to her than a troop of Germans singing in the street, when the breathing of her classmates hurt her eardrums, though the teacher was inaudible. Of course, the question of night time air raids was something else altogether: no one was sure about raids anymore.

She rolled over in bed, her gaze fixed on the bars of light that spilled through the shutters and onto the walls. She was so happy to be home, in her room with the red wallpaper, with the miniature armoire below the built in bookshelves, with her own books, her own outgrown dolls, her pens and her notes and the curtain with its pattern of violets. The room was too small for anything but her bed, the armoire and a three-legged stool. Jeanine's was much bigger, though she was the baby, but it could only be reached through Maman's room and anyway Yvonne preferred this one with its lovely red wallpaper, its balcony overlooking the street.

She and Jeanine had been sent home from school along with the other boarders: the Allies were expected any day now and it would be better for families to be together. When she'd heard the news, Yvonne cheered out loud right in the middle of Latin. Boarders wouldn't have to take exams; they wouldn't have to obey the nuns again until September. Not all of the nuns were vicious—two or three, beloved of the younger girls, were even pretty—but they were all part of the same terrible regimen. When the Germans came, her grandmother pointed out at Sunday dinner that some of them weren't so bad after all, some had perfectly decent manners, and her father left the table in disgust; Yvonne, allying herself with her father for the first and only time in her life, had thought, *it's the same with the nuns. It's stupid to make distinctions between them.*

She hated the nuns frankly and openly as she was able to do because of the coal rations her father gave to the convent, and her boldness filled the other girls with awe, but Yvonne tried not to bask in their admiration: if it weren't for the coal, she'd be as big a coward as the next girl; she had no illusions about her own strength.

When she was twelve, the Mother Superior had asked her—sitting above Yvonne in the damp room with the green curtains, a room that smelled of creosote and old upholstery—"What are you thinking, my child?" Yvonne, whose knees ached against the stone floor, glanced up at the window and saw through a crack in the curtains that the sky was blue and windy. "I would like to crush you," she said. "I am thinking of how much I would like to crush you." She made a motion with her hands as if she were grinding something with a mortar and pestle. The Mother Superior said nothing. Her face was stuck in its wimple like a face locked in the stocks. Yvonne felt as if she might be sick, but she didn't stand up and the Mother Superior did not move. She hardly seemed to breathe, sitting there with her wide eyes and her wide, white face. When Yvonne at last unfolded herself to leave, her knees were bruised, but still the Mother Superior hadn't spoken.

And though for days she was afraid she had committed a mortal sin and worried that she'd lost God's love forever, nothing was ever said or done to punish her. It was as if the moment had never happened, as if she'd dreamed it; as, for all she knew, she had dreamed last night's sirens.

She stared at the red walls—so deep and rich a red, it looked like velvet—and at the bars of light that fell across the walls like strokes of heat, of actual fire.

Any minute now, Maman would call her down to breakfast, and what was the point? A watery bowl of Caffix that satisfied no craving. Why go down when her room, even with the shutters closed, was so beautiful and was hers alone? She wanted to open her shutters and breathe in the sweet salt air, the smell of honeysuckle and seagulls, of the dusty pear trees across the road; but then everyone would know she was awake and there would be no excuse for staying in bed. And even with the shutters closed, her room was beautiful beyond words. She gazed up at the spines of her books and the molding along the tops of the walls, at Mirabelle's lone porcelain foot sticking out from beneath her petticoat. Mirabelle sat up with the books, placed with the other M's (Moliere, Montesquieu) to keep things in alphabetical order. A slip of sunlight lit up her white frills and below her, in the semi-darkness, gleamed the small armoire, with its *fleur de lis*, its fluted edges—who had done this, Yvonne wondered, carved the wood so beautifully, polished it to such a luster? On the rickety stool was an old lamp and even it, with its shade partly burnt through, seemed to Yvonne a kind of miracle.

Her throat tightened. Surely she would see him today. Why shouldn't he bicycle down the street at 2:00 as he had always done and glance up at her balcony? She didn't know his name. She didn't even know where he had been headed every day last summer when he rode past, staring up at her. For weeks she hadn't met his gaze. She would catch sight of him, turning the corner onto their street—always between 1:50 and 2:05—his head bare, red hair ruffled by the breeze and his face open, handsome, easy. One arm dangled by his side and the other barely touched the handlebar. Instantly she glanced down and though she felt his eyes on her, felt the heat of his gaze the entire length of time it took for him to ride down to the end of the street—a one-minute ride that seemed sometimes to take hours—she couldn't have known in the beginning if he even saw her. When he was right below the house, she saw a blur of him in her peripheral vision, but that was all.

And then one day—her heart had been sore all morning, like something she'd swallowed the wrong way—she glanced out just when he would be approaching the house and there he was, below her, staring up. She looked at him with the same degree of terror and nausea she had felt when she'd spoken to the Mother Superior, but the next day she did it again. And then for days, weeks, she didn't look away at all but stared at him frankly the whole length of his ride and he stared back, turning to look over his shoulder when he reached the end of the street. They were the happiest days of her life, of all her sixteen years, those two weeks when, for a minute or two every afternoon, she and the red-haired boy stared so nakedly at each other.

She didn't eat even when she could have, and the feel of her bones pressing up through her skin thrilled her. Hipbones, clavicle, collar bone, jaw bone: wherever her skin grew taut, she imagined his hand. The world was glazed with light and the Germans made no sound at all. *I love you,* she thought, watching him ride towards her. And even when he wasn't there: *I love you, I love you, I love you.*

She heard his voice sometimes. Once when she was coming out of the bathroom, once while she was waiting in line at the *cremerie.* It was deep and low and always a shade too close, but she forgave him: he would speak more softly if he knew it hurt her. Like sandpaper on an open sore. She hadn't known that pleasure and fear were so alike.

But she was never afraid when she saw him. She stared right into his eyes, which were the color of the first blue of morning, and smiled at him.

And then one day, he stopped. He parked his bike in front of her house and called up to her. "Hello!" he said, his voice so much milder than she had imagined. He bowed. She stifled a laugh—great beads of sweat were rolling down her sides and she was trembling all over—and called back: "Hello!"

That was the end of it, of course: her father burst out the front door, told the boy to stop gawking like an idiot, went upstairs and slapped Yvonne across the face, in full view of the street. She never dared to meet his gaze again, though for the rest of the summer she still stood on the balcony every day from 1:30 to 2:05, her mouth dry and her throat sore, but her eyes downcast. She prayed for him to look up at her, to see her suffering, to know that she loved him. But now, though she could hear the whisper of his tires on the pavement as he came down the street, she no longer felt his gaze. He might have been looking at her and he might not. She didn't know. At the end of the summer, the day before she went back to school, she let herself glance out at him for an instant. He was not looking at her. He kept his eyes downcast so that he wouldn't have seen if anything was coming towards him, and so that she couldn't see his face. But suddenly he paused in front of her house again. He slipped something under a rock, righted his bicycle, and vanished.

That the evening, just before curfew, when the street was nearly dark, she slipped out and found his note. *You are a bird.*

That was all. She read it over and over and gave it a thousand meanings, seeing in the slope of his letters such declarations of love, such caresses, but that's all it was, the three words, *t'es un oiseau.* The *tu* was everything, as if they'd already kissed, as if he had already cupped his hand around the back of her neck and pulled her towards him, felt the dampness of her skin and pressed his lips against hers, as if she had already smelled him, felt the coolness of his body, the muscles of his hands, as if she had felt her teeth press against the inside of her lips as they did when she pressed her own palm to her mouth, imagining. The *tu* and the bird, that she was a bird, that he should say so, the knowledge of her so intimate, plunging into her stomach, but what could she say in return? She stayed up late, composing a long letter in which she described not only the depth of her love but all the members of her family and the color of her room and her hatred of the Germans and all the things they would eat together, the two of them, when the war was over. The letter was seventeen pages long and it was three in the morning before she finished it and then she folded it up and hid it in a notebook. She took a clean sheet of paper, wrote *Thank you,* and, though it would kill her father to know that she was violating the curfew—putting them all at risk for her own selfish purposes!—she slipped through the front door and left the note under the same rock where he had left his.

"Yvonne!" her mother called. "Are you still asleep?"

She closed her eyes, seeing against her eyelids the beautiful bars of light, the deep red of the wallpaper.

"Coming!"

And then, because it was hopeless, they'd call her down no matter what now, she rose and opened her shutters and gasped at the freshness of the air, the smell of the salt, of the honeysuckle. It was not possible that the world could be so beautiful. She closed the curtains so that she could dress, and then, opening them again, let the light flood into the room: the walls turned crimson and the armoire glowed like roasting chestnuts—none of this was possible, none of it. She made up her bed, smoothing the violets on her bedspread with the flat of her palm and this, too—the bed, the motion of her own hand, seemed impossibly beautiful to her.

But Maman was waiting downstairs with a list of chores and Yvonne must hurry or be met already—so soon into her vacation—with her mother's disapproval. (Because surely they wouldn't call the girls back to school now? Surely this was the beginning of summer vacation. Either the Allies would come and there'd be too much fighting, or they wouldn't and everyone would keep expecting them from day to day.) It was as if Maman had suffered a stroke when she was displeased, her face suddenly frozen and remote.

She hurried downstairs, hurried in the bathroom (and everywhere such beauty: the way the banister reflected the light; the small octagonal window in the bathroom opening to the salty breeze.)

Her mother and Jeanine were sitting at the table drinking their bowls of Caffix. Papa was already in the garden—weeding?—and it struck Yvonne that, though she had wanted to stay in her room, though the red of her walls was like the inside of a rose, and she had not wanted to be called down to breakfast, even this—the long table, the bowls of foul liquid, her mother's sagging face and her father's shadow through the window—was more beautiful than she had ever realized. Fourteen years old, Jeanine slurped her Caffix, long brown braids falling down her back, her chair a little closer to Maman's than it needed to be. She was mostly fun, cheerfully laughing at Yvonne's jokes and a willing slave when she was small, but she still clung to Maman, always standing just slightly behind and next to her, always pulling in her chair a little closer than necessary; and Maman relied on Jeanine as she had never relied on Yvonne, asking her to fetch things, to help with this or that chore even when Jeanine had schoolwork to do, to unfasten the back of her dress, fetch the cream for her feet.

Maman smiled up at Yvonne, wearily; she was always weary nowadays. "What a beautiful day, isn't? I thought we'd weed the lawn around the steps."

"We might die today," Yvonne said, breezily.

Jeanine, half asleep, kept her head over her bowl of Caffix, forcing the hot liquid down with tiny, labored sips.

"Did you hear the sirens?" Maman asked.

"I think so."

"I thought so, too," Maman said, putting down her napkin though her Caffix was only half drunk. "Brush your teeth, girls, and then we'll get to work."

And though it was a long time to lunch, and longer still until the hour between one and two when the family rested and Yvonne stood out on her balcony, she did not mind weeding today. The sun warmed the top of her head, and Jeanine hummed mindlessly and all the flowers were blooming, the roses and the peonies and the foxglove. The heads of lettuce were full and healthy, all in their rows, and the sweet peas covered the fences. She remembered the poem she'd memorized for English, *the lark's on the wing....all's right with the world*, and, resting on her haunches, looking up at the warm, blue sky, she thought, *Yes. It is.* She would see him today.

Though the war raged on, though all she wanted was a fistful of butter, though every day, instead of food, the shops filled up with Germans, still the sky shone and the roses grew against the garden wall. And Maman, sweating beneath her sun hat, wordlessly taking the shears from Jeanine, was beautiful, with her fat knees, her rings of sweat. Even Papa, digging at the far side of the yard, with his cold face, his insistence on work as the cure for all evil, was beautiful. For she was loved.

She gazed at the colors that rose suddenly from the garden wall when, meaning to water the flowers, she watered the stones instead, and at the rabbit hutch with its dark, musty smell, so redolent of stew, of the rabbits' tiny pelts stitched together into coats, their bodies smooth and shiny after they'd been skinned. It horrified her in the first winter of the war that Papa killed them and that she herself was required to skin them; the first several times she'd wept, with Maman standing over her, correcting her technique— you must pull just so so that the skin comes off in one piece—but now all she thought of was the warm, slippery meat, the soft fur, the glistening bodies, and this was not only because she was in love, but because she was ravenous after her bowl of Caffix and a morning outside. And because no matter how warm she grew working in the garden, she would never forget the cold of the winter, or the chilblains she could never scratch hard enough.

For lunch they had omelets and salad, though there was no oil for the dressing, no butter for the eggs. But now she didn't mind, her heart racing: soon they would all take their naps, and she could go out onto her balcony.

"I'd like to talk to you both after lunch," Maman said to Yvonne and Jeanine.

Yvonne's palms grew damp. "I'm so tired, Maman," she said, dry-mouthed, her throat so tight it hurt to speak. "Could we talk later?"

"Well, of course," said Maman. "Let's all have a nap."

Her head ached, and her throat, her heart, and the minutes passed more slowly than when, as a small child, she had waited in the schoolyard for her mother to pick her up for lunch.

The clock struck the quarter hour and Yvonne jumped, her eyes fixed on the end of the street.

The hour came, the quarter past. He was not coming.

Maman knocked on her door. "It's late, Yvonne." And in her mother's voice, she heard the truth: they would all be dead soon. Maman had known what she was waiting for; had given her the extra fifteen minutes so that she could die happy. Maman could not have known that he wasn't coming, that—what? He'd found another girl? Moved away, died? Maman wouldn't have been watching the street all these weeks and months, she would simply have known that Yvonne would watch it as soon as she came home, and Maman would have allowed her, because they were dying; when you were dying, you could do anything.

But he hadn't come. She had waited faithfully, and he had forgotten her. She would die without him—her body revolted as if she'd swallowed poison: she couldn't die. Then she began to laugh, a trembling so fine it was barely more than a hum. What choice was there? Soon—in a week? A few hours?—she would simply cease.

The world had seemed so vivid that morning only because she was dying. For though she had loved the boy with the red hair, though it had been delicious to feel herself loved—*t'es un oiseau*—still, the sudden beauty of the walls, of the polished wood, of her mother's sweat-stained dress—what were they but the rapture of farewell?

"I'll be right there, Maman." She turned from the balcony and, without thinking, almost pulled the shutters closed, the windows, as if it were time for bed. Her chest burned, but her mother was waiting for her, with her kind, sagging face, her fat arms. Yvonne opened the door, and there was Maman, white with irritation. She wasn't thinking of death at all.

Yvonne's eyes stung. The boy with the red hair did not love her, her mother's face was stiff and disapproving as a nun's (more so, because no one paid Maman off for Yvonne's lack of self-discipline.) They would be dead soon and everyone went on with his chores, as if it were a day like any other, as if it meant nothing at all to leave the honeysuckle, the sea cliffs, the footless leg of Mirabelle.

"It's too late to have the talk I wanted to have with you," Maman said, grimly. "Papa wants to you to get right to your schoolwork."

Yvonne, wondering what in the world Maman would have wanted to talk to her about, since apparently she realized neither that Yvonne was in love, nor that they were going to be killed soon—her behavior at school? The need to economize? The coming chores?—reached up on impulse and put her palm to Maman's cheek. "I'm sorry I overslept, petite Maman," she said, and kissed her.

Maybe it was better this way, with no one knowing, and once again she could hardly breathe, the house was so beautiful, the garden, the stone steps outside the door turning white in the sunlight.

Papa sat with her and Jeanine at the dining room table and watched over them while they studied so that their eyes would not stray to the open windows. Montaigne said, *My life has been filled with terrible misfortune, most of which never happened,* and the smell of the garden washed over her and she glanced at the dark hairs on the backs of Papa's hands and the dark braids down Jeanine's back—how steadily they both read—and she would have kissed them too except that she didn't want to startle them.

In the night, hearing bombs and sure they wouldn't live till morning, Yvonne crawled into her mother's bed.

"What is it?" Maman asked sleepily.

"I was afraid."

"Yvonne?" Maman asked, waking fully. "I thought you were Jeanine. What are you doing here?"

"A bad dream."

"Sh-sh," said Maman. "You're too big." But she put her arm around Yvonne and Yvonne curled into her soft, faintly sour body.

The next day dawned as beautifully as the last, and Yvonne, waking in the room she loved so much, saw no reason why they should die that day or why the boy with the red hair, belatedly learning that the convent had sent all its pupils home, should not come by after all.

She went down gaily to her bowl of Caffix and gaily refused to brush her teeth after, because, as she said, they'd certainly be killed today, and Maman, with circles under her eyes, rolled her eyes but said nothing except that they had an awful lot of work to do. The windows hadn't been washed in two months and there was a rabbit to kill.

Yvonne stood on the little balcony after lunch, staring down to the end of the street, and though she imagined a dozen perfectly good reasons he might not show up—why should he have heard that the convent had sent all the girls home?—her arms trembled at her sides and she felt as if she would be sick.

The clock struck one thirty and though he had never come that early, not once, the sound of the planes overhead became confused in her mind with the whisper of his bicycle tires so that it was only as the flames, bursting through the red walls, singed her back, that she gave up hoping it was he.

Then she

Then then

her; she had not taken her eyes
there who blinks or swallows in
hadn't come. She would die who him
ed as if she'd swallowed
ed, feathers, her bones turned
ty wasn't capable of it.

to begin she didn't know then,
begin. She began to laugh then,
was, true?
into a ~~house~~ barely more than a did she
with sweat. What choice ~~did~~
She cold be dead. The shock of it,
what did it matter what? who this matter?
The red-haired boy.

then that the mons's rapture had
had been abt death. It Magh she
she had been compared to a
birds, still. The beauty of the walls, the polished wood, other
mother's sweat-stained dress — what was that but the
rapture of farewell?

she indulse
not been abt love,
had loved a been fighter, though
sore, as if she'd swallow
"I'll be right there, Maman."
Above that the chest was
somely the wrong way, but what was that compared to all
awaited her beyond the door. Her mother's kind, soft's face,
steam's stairwell, the garden beyond, Harianne, Papa,
t all she wanted was to throw herself into her w
arms.

Her mother stood on the other side of the door, ex
beyond words. She wasn't thinking of death at a

THE FIRST STORY

The joke is, if I had a kid who wrote the kinds of things I wrote when I was little, I'd be in a blind panic. Eight years old, and I'm sitting in my parents' living room, listening to Simon and Garfunkel's bleaker songs ("I am a Rock," "Richard Corey") bawling my eyes out and writing poems about tears, rain and a man who goes home and puts a bullet in his head. It's funnier than it sounds only because I'm not depressed, I'm just deeply moved by pathos. And I want to be older. I love my life, but I also like the sophisticated portrait of grief contained in those songs. This is no playground meltdown, this is how grownups suffer. (It's 1968, and when Gene McCarthy loses out at the Chicago Democratic Convention, I'll wear a black armband like my teenage sister's.)

Readers of my fiction might argue that I never outgrew my fascination with darkness and it's true that my characters suffer, but what interests me is finding moments of light in their suffering. There's no darkness so absolute that it doesn't contain some light; if the writer's task is to reveal that—as I believe it is—we can't shy away from the dark. We can't sustain or console our readers—be *generous* writers—if we're squeamish about pain. I'm not sure "Richard Corey" is truly revelatory, but another Simon and Garfunkel song, "Save the Life of my Child," is: in it, a boy is about to jump to his death from a tall building; a crowd of adults waits below in horror and fascination. Just when the onlookers reach a fevered pitch, the boy leaps off his ledge—and flies away. The last line of the song, repeated over and over as the boy vanishes, is "oh my grace, I've got no hiding place."

I love everything about that song: the unexpected liberation of a boy we think is doomed, the unexpected beauty in a scene that starts out so ugly, with a crowd of breathless adults just waiting for him to fall. I love the possibility of flight not just as a means of escape but as an indication of what, were we not bowed down with fear, we'd all be capable of. And I love the last line. I love its suggestion that that's all the boy ever wanted—all, perhaps, any teenager wants: privacy, a place of his or her own, a place to hide from the fascinated condemnation of adults. But I also love the deeper truth it contains: we cannot hide before God (to whom, after all, the line is addressed) and this is no cause for shame, but for the greatest freedom. It doesn't matter to me whether his flight is a metaphor for death; I took it literally when I was eight, and I take it literally still: in this world or the next, that boy is flying.

When I was little—and, really, still—I was drawn to hiding places; and in conversations, I never wanted to reveal too much. The anguish and longing in those words—*I've got no hiding place*—spoke to me; the wild possibility that this might be good gave me courage.

As readers, we're heartened when we come to a line and think, *yes, that's it, that's exactly what I've felt.* That thrill of recognition—*I'm not alone*—changes our life; and it's a sense of *being* recognized, as if the author had seen *us*, rather than vice versa. (We might or might not feel as if we know the author, but I think what we crave most is being seen and understood.) The thrill is greatest when what the author has recognized in us is a feeling or sensation we didn't even know we had. Part of our heart that was previously mysterious to us is illuminated, and we're less hidden from ourselves.

To illuminate is to create: In the beginning was the Word, and then there was Light, in the Bible, and in every Western story since. The first books I read, the books that made me want to write, were *Dick and Jane.* The sun-drenched grass those children played in was paradise, the sentences below the grass a shimmering truth. In school, we spent hours writing Dick and Jane style phrases over and over, until we could form our letters perfectly. *I see a cat. I see a cat. I see a cat.* (I might go on to write poems about my tears like rain, but of my early works, it's those clear, lovely, cursive words I am most proud.) We also wrote *I am.* Over and over: *I am.* What we knew best was that, like God, we *were.*

As I grew older, of course, it was stories of the fallen world that drew me, stories that considered what was possible after we'd discovered our failings—how we might be both broken and radiant. I read voraciously, deliciously, until I got to college where, in grim pursuit of good grades, I started reading by the clock. Counting how many words of a text I could read in an hour, I figured my schedule accordingly and took my books to the science library, where the fluorescent lights buzzed all night long and the focused calculations of my fellow students kept me alert. One night at 2 AM I sat in a cubicle chewing my pen and reading *Paradise Lost;* all around me I could hear the rapid clicking of calculators. I came to the end of the poem, where Adam and Eve, having forfeited everything, must now fend for themselves: "The world was all before them…They hand in hand with wandring steps and slow/Through Eden took their solitary way." I burst into loud, gulping sobs. Who knows what the young chemists and physicists and mathematicians all around me thought. What I was thinking was, *this, yes— however we've failed, the question is, what will we do* next? *How can we go forward?* (And look how beautiful the world is, even now.) I sat in that buzzing cubicle and I couldn't stop crying.

Freedom, the ordinary resurrection of people making the most of things when all seems lost, the possibility of forgiveness—these are the subjects that keep me reading, but, of course, they're all meaningless without guilt.

Writers have a lot to feel guilty about—the suffering we have to explore is not just what we've lived and seen, but also what we've caused *by writing.* We're thieves at every turn: we "borrow" from Genesis and every other text we've heard or read, justifying ourselves on the grounds that each new story is a re-interpretation. Worse, we steal from our most innocent loved ones along with total strangers. We use their stories, their physical features, their accents, their desires and their secrets to animate our fiction. The hottest and most valuable items are the tics and fears they're not even aware they possess—these are the things that make fiction believable, that lead our readers (especially ones we've never met) to say how deeply understood they felt by what we wrote. How *seen*. Again, we justify: it's mostly our own desires and sorrows and tics and fears we harvest for our characters. That's true. But we're still kleptomaniacs everywhere we go. We can't ride the subway or share a meal with a friend without taking stock of details we might use: how our friend holds her fork, for example. Just that.

Like other criminals, we stand apart, casing the joint. Watching out for the hidden story, the priceless line, we don't quite lose ourselves in the event—and so, along with theft and indiscretion, we're guilty of survival. Surviving's good—I recommend it, and recommend observing like a writer in *order* to survive—but still, the guilt's inevitable. Everyone else is devastated by a flood, and we're thinking of how best to describe it.

Genesis has a lot to say about guilt, but Genesis isn't my only source. Each of us has our own private creation myth, the story we grew up with—how our parents met or what happened the day we were born—which colors all our writing. Mine is D-day.

My mother is French, of the generation whose adolescence *was* World War II. She has the most beautiful voice I've ever heard and she's a great storyteller. Listening to her was my favorite thing to do when I was small; I wanted to hear everything over and over: how she and her family stayed warm through the brutal, impoverished winters; the time she stayed out past curfew, but made it home without encountering any Nazis; the Jewish child a neighbor saved from a roundup, claiming he was hers; a Jewish uncle whose painting saved him from the camps. All happy stories of survival, in which the dead play no part.

But there was this one, too:

My mother and her family were living in Normandy in 1944. My mother, studying to be a physicist, traveled back and forth between the University of Paris and her hometown of Caen every week. It was a risky trip to make: in order to disrupt the transport of Nazi supplies, the Allies were regularly bombing the trains. But my mother kept right on commuting.

On June 4th, she left for Paris for a week of exams; on the 6th, the Allies bombed her home. Her mother, grandmother and sixteen-year-old sister were buried in the rubble; her stepfather and fifteen-year-old sister were in the garden, weeding, and survived.

My mother's youngest sister has never spoken of D-day, but from her stepfather, my mother learned a few details: Nicolette, the beautiful, rebellious sister who died, had refused to brush her teeth that morning. There were rumors that the Allies would liberate them any day and when her mother asked her if she'd brushed her teeth, my aunt just laughed: "Why should I? We'll probably die today anyway."

My step-grandfather and my younger aunt spent weeks digging the family from the rubble; they had heard my grandmother and great-grandmother crying out beneath the weight of the beams and stones, but by the time they reached them, they were dead. Of Nicolette, all they ever found was an arm.

Nicolette's arm, her beauty, her unbrushed teeth—these were the details that held me transfixed, and though it was a terrible story, my mother's voice was so musical that I could not hear it enough. It was how I thought the world began: a downpour of bombs, fire, and emerging from that wreckage the image of my dark-haired aunt as she is in a photograph from earlier in the summer: there is her smile, there her smooth young arm which is how I always pictured it when my mother told the story: not blasted and decaying, but whole and lovely, with its graceful hand holding a book.

In the picture, you can't see the book's cover, but I imagine it's a volume of poetry, because that's part of the story, too: a day or so before she died, my rebel aunt, who refused to brush her teeth, copied down lines from one of her favorite English poems: "the lark's on the wing….all's right with the world."

In my mind, after the rain of bombs, after all those deaths, there's just my aunt's young, slim arm, left behind like a forgotten handkerchief—some beautiful, delicate thing—a scented note: *All's right with the world.*

Because there's my mother, telling me the story—my mother, whose body and voice are all I need of paradise when I'm small—and here we are in prosperous 1960's America: out of the chaos and darkness of World War II, such light, such order. There are snakes in the garden, too: all war stories are shadowed with moral dilemmas, with questions about how we *might* behave, were we hungry or scared or desperate enough. But in my mother's presence, there's just peace.

As I get older, those snakey questions trouble me more, work their way into my writing—who's good? Who's bad? Who's responsible?—and D-day remains a central image in everything I write. In my first novel, D-day's the turning point: half-way through, several of the major characters visit a house in Normandy; I kill some, let others survive and that sets in motion the story's unfolding. In my second novel, I create a whole family out of the rubble: an American soldier sees a young French girl digging for her family, gets her pregnant and—if she'll agree to give up their bastard child and start over—offers to marry her.

If I were my mother's youngest sister, I wouldn't like my writing. I've tried to be respectful: Even "Liberation," my most "factual" story, makes no claim to be anything but fiction. I don't know what my aunt Nicolette was thinking about the day she died; I only know what my fictional character, Yvonne, was thinking—Yvonne who, like all my characters, is a version of myself. Still. At fifteen, my aunt dug through the ruins of her house to find her mother, her grandmother and her sister. She doesn't speak of it, and she and I don't talk about my work. This is the dark side of writing, for which there is no answer.

What *would* I have done if I'd been in a war? I don't know, but I am sure of this: I'd steal every apple in the garden, without any prompting from a snake.

For all my brazen stealing, I know this, too: it *is* only ever my own heart I'm laying bare, as if I could belatedly atone for standing apart. For my urge to hide. When I do that and a reader in some other room, some other town, feels seen—when she glimpses possibilities as surprising as forgiveness, as lovely as flight—the boundaries between us dissolve: we're like lovers at a masked ball, half hidden, half exposed, light-filled beneath the cover of darkness.

BARK

Cathy Smith Bowers

There is evidence, scientists
say, that before dogs
were domesticated, before
we rescued them from wilderness,

they howled, growled, yelped,
and whined, but did not bark.
Evidence, they say,
that hearing human

speech—*beg   sit   stay*—they
tried to mimic it
and got the bark instead.
Lost darling, casualty of my divorce,

surest way my husband knew
to punish me (so loved I named
you Seamus, Mr. Heaney to strangers
and acquaintances) remember

the night I fetched you
from your pen, the hurricane
already moving inward from the coast,
how you mistook my cautionary

measure for some midnight jamboree,
soiree du chien in celebration
of something you couldn't quite remember
but must have done right that day.

That night you were too happy
to bark, pranced in jubilation
of your middle-of-the-night reprieve
around and around the couch

where at either end my husband
and I dozed in the ostensible safety
of our living room. We had learned
already the democracy of those storms.

Three years before, our yard
untouched, every oak and hemlock
pointing as ever upward, as we stared
at our neighbor's property

reduced to sticks and stones.
Not knowing what other storms
were gathering, you continued
your solitary parade around

the room, where at intervals
we would feel against our drowsy lips
that unschooled kiss, the sudden unabashed
joy of your wet tongue. Years later,

over drinks or in the grocery
checkout line, friends catching up
on the progress of our families, how suddenly
embarrassed and put off they become

when I pull out pictures of you
and the wag-tail ghost of your name
lopes across my tongue. Then the sob,
the yelp, the whine. Almost a bark.

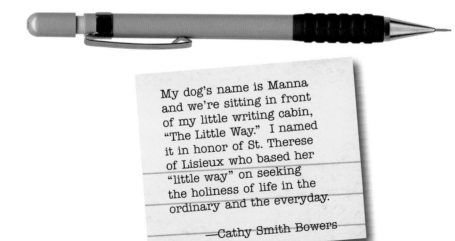

My dog's name is Manna
and we're sitting in front
of my little writing cabin,
"The Little Way." I named
it in honor of St. Therese
of Lisieux who based her
"little way" on seeking
the holiness of life in the
ordinary and the everyday.

—Cathy Smith Bowers

EXCUSES

(An excerpt from *Teacher Man*)
Frank McCourt

Mikey Dolan handed me a note from his mother explaining his absence the day before:

Dear Mr. McCort, Mikey's grandmother who is my mother eighty years of age fell down the stairs from too much coffee and I kept Mikey at home to take care of her and his baby sister so I could go to my job at the coffee shop in the ferry terminal. Please excuse Mikey and he'll do his best in the future as he likes your class. Sincerely yours, Imelda Dolan. PS. His grandmother is OK.

When Mikey handed me the note, so blatantly forged under my nose, I said nothing. I had seen him writing it at his desk with his left hand to disguise his own handwriting, which, because of his years in Catholic primary schools, was the best in the class. The nuns didn't care whether you went to heaven or hell or married a Protestant as long as your handwriting was clear and handsome and if you were weak in that department they'd bend your thumbs back till you screamed for mercy and promised a calligraphy that would open the doors of heaven. Also, if you wrote with the left hand, it was clear proof you were born with a Satanic streak and it was the business of the sisters to bend your thumbs, even here in America, land of the free and home of the brave.

So, there was Mikey, laboring with his left hand to disguise his exquisite Catholic calligraphy. This was not his first time forging a note but I said nothing because most of the parental-excuse notes in my desk drawer were written by the boys and girls of McKee Vocational and Technical High School and if I were to confront each forger I'd be busy twenty-four hours a day. It would also lead to indignation, hurt feelings and strained relations between them and me.

I said to one boy, Did your mother really write this note, Danny?

He was defensive, hostile. Yeah, my mother wrote it.

It's a nice note, Danny. She writes well.

McKee students were proud of their mothers and only a lout would let that compliment pass without thanks.

He said thanks, and returned to his seat.

I could have asked him if the note was his but I knew better. I liked him and didn't want him sullen in the third row. He'd tell classmates I suspected him and that might make them sullen, too, because they'd been forging excuse notes since they learned to write and years later they don't want to be bothered by teachers suddenly getting moral.

An excuse note is just a part of school life. Everyone knows they're fiction, so what's the big deal?

Parents getting kids out of the house in the morning have little time for writing notes that they know will wind up in the school garbage anyway. They're so harried they'll say, Oh, you need an excuse note for yesterday, honey? Write it yourself and I'll sign it. They sign it without even looking at it and the sad part is they don't know what they're missing. If they could read those notes they'd discover their kids are capable of the finest American prose: fluent, imaginative, clear, dramatic, fantastic, focused, persuasive, useful.

I threw Mikey's note into a desk drawer along with dozens of others: notes written on every size and color of paper, scrawled, scratched, stained. While my classes took a test that day I began to read notes I had only glanced at before. I made two piles, one for the genuine notes written by mothers, the other for forgeries. The second was the larger pile, with writing that ranged from imaginative to lunatic.

I was having an epiphany. I always wondered what an epiphany would be like and now I knew. I wondered also why I'd never had this particular epiphany before.

Isn't it remarkable, I thought, how they resist any kind of writing assignment in class or at home. They whine and say they're busy and it's hard putting two hundred words together on any subject. But when they forge these excuse notes they're brilliant. Why? I have a drawer full of excuse notes that could be turned into an anthology of Great American Excuses or Great American Lies.

The drawer was filled with samples of American talent never mentioned in song, story or scholarly study. How could I have ignored this treasure trove, these gems of fiction, fantasy, creativity, crawthumping, self-pity, family problems, boilers exploding, ceilings collapsing, fires sweeping whole blocks, babies and pets pissing on homework, unexpected births, heart attacks, strokes, miscarriages, robberies? Here was American high school writing at its best-raw, real, urgent, lucid, brief, lying:

The stove caught fire and the wallpaper went up and the fire department kept us out of the house all night.

The toilet was blocked and we had to go down the street to the Kilkenny Bar where my cousin works to use their toilet but that was blocked too from the night before and you can imagine how hard it was for my Ronnie to get ready for school. I hope you'll excuse him this one time and it won't happen again. The man at the Kilkenny Bar was very nice on account of how he knows your brother, Mr. McCord.

Arnold doesn't have his work today because he was getting off the train yesterday and the door closed on his school bag and the train took it away. He yelled to the conductor who said very vulgar things as the train drove away. Something should be done.

His sister's dog ate his homework and I hope it chokes him.

Her baby brother peed on her story when she was in the bathroom this morning.

A man died in the bathtub upstairs and it overflowed and messed up all Roberta's homework on the table.

Her big brother got mad at her and threw her essay out the window and it flew away allover Staten Island which is not a good thing because people will read it and get the wrong impression unless they read the ending which explains everything.

He had the composition you told him to write but he was going over it on the ferry and a big wind came and blowed it away.

We were evicted from our apartment and the mean sheriff said if my son kept yelling for his notebook he'd have us all arrested.

I imagined the writers of excuse notes on buses, trains, ferries, in coffee shops, on park benches, trying to discover new and logical excuses, trying to write as they thought their parents would.

They didn't know that honest excuse notes from parents were usually dull. "Peter was late because the alarm clock did not go off." A note like that didn't even merit a place in the trash can.

Toward the end of the term I typed a dozen excuse notes on a stencil and distributed them to my two senior classes. They read, silently and intently.

Yo, Mr. McCourt, what's this?

Excuse notes.

Whaddya mean, excuse notes? Who wrote them?

You did, or some of you did. I omitted the names to protect the guilty. They're supposed to be written by parents, but you and I know the real authors. Yes, Mikey?

So, what are we supposed to do with these excuse notes?

We'll read them aloud. I want you to realize this is the first class in the world ever to study the art of the excuse note, the first class, ever, to practice writing them. You are so lucky to have a teacher like me who has taken your best writing, the excuse note, and turned it into a subject worthy of study.

They're smiling. They know. We're in this together. Sinners.

Some of the notes on that sheet were written by people in this class. You know who you are. You used your imagination and didn't settle for the old alarm-clock story. You'll be making excuses the rest of your life and you'll want them to be believable and original. You might even wind up writing excuses for your own children when they're late or absent or up to some devilment. Try it now. Imagine you have a fifteen-year-old son or daughter who needs an excuse for falling behind in English. Let it rip.

They didn't look around. They didn't chew on their pens. They didn't dawdle. They were eager, desperate to make up excuses for their fifteen-year-old sons and daughters. It was an act of loyalty and love and, you never know, some day they might need these notes.

They produced a rhapsody of excuses, ranging from a family epidemic of diarrhea to a sixteen-wheeler truck crashing into a house, to a severe case of food poisoning blamed on the McKee High School cafeteria.

They said, More, more. Could we do more?

I was taken aback. How do I handle this enthusiasm?

There was another epiphany or a flash of inspiration or illumination or something. I went to the board and wrote: "For Homework Tonight."

That was a mistake. The word homework carries negative connotations. I erased it and they said, Yeah, yeah.

I told them, You can start it here in class and continue at home or on the other side of the moon. What I'd like you to write is ...

I wrote it on the board: "An Excuse Note from Adam to God" or "An Excuse Note from Eve to God."

The heads went down. Pens raced across paper. They could do this with one hand tied behind their backs. With their eyes closed. Secret smiles around the room. Oh, this is a good one, baby, and we know what's coming, don't we? Adam blames Eve. Eve blames Adam. They both blame God or

Lucifer. Blame all around except for God, who has the upper hand and kicks them out of Eden so that their descendants wind up in McKee Vocational and Technical High School writing excuse notes for the Erst man and woman, and maybe God Himself needs an excuse note for some of His big mistakes.

The bell rang, and for the first time in my three and a half years of teaching, I saw high school students so immersed they had to be urged out of the room by friends hungry for lunch.

Yo, Lenny. Come on. Finish it in the cafeteria.

Next day everyone had excuse notes, not only from Adam and Eve but from God and Lucifer, some compassionate, some nasty. On behalf of Eve, Lisa Quinn defended her seduction of Adam on the grounds that she was tired of lying around Paradise doing nothing day in, day out. She was also tired of God sticking His nose into their business and never allowing them a moment of privacy. It was all right for Him. He could go off and hide behind a cloud somewhere and roar from time to time if He saw her or Adam go near his precious apple tree.

There are heated discussions about the relative guilt and sinfulness of Adam and Eve. It is agreed, unanimously, that Lucifer the Snake is a bastard, a son of a bitch and no good. No one is so brave as to say anything negative about God although there are hints and suggestions He could have been a little more understanding of the plight of the First Man and the First Woman.

Mikey Dolan says you could never talk like this in Catholic schools. Jesus (sorry), the nuns would pull you out of your seat by the ears and have your parents in to explain where you got ideas that were pure blasphemy.

Other boys in the class, non-Catholics, brag they'd never put up with that bullshit. They'd knock the nuns on their ass and how come all them Catholic boys were such sissies?

The discussion was drifting and I worried that details might get back to Catholic parents who would object to a mention of nuns being treated roughly. I asked them to think about anyone in the world at present or in history who could use a good excuse note.

I wrote the suggestions on the blackboard:

Eva Braun, Hitler's girlfriend.

I asked, How about Hitler himself?

Naw, naw, never. No excuses there.

But maybe he had a miserable childhood.

They wouldn't agree. An excuse note for Hitler might be a great challenge for a writer but the excuse would never come from this class.

On the board: Julius and Ethel Rosenberg, executed in 1953 for treason.

How about excuse notes for draft dodgers?

Oh, yeah, Mr. McCourt. These guys have big excuse notes. They don't wanna fight for their country but that's not us.

On the board: Judas, Attila the Hun, Lee Harvey Oswald, Al Capone, all the politicians in America.

Yo, Mr. McCourt, could you put teachers up there? Not you but all these pain-in-the-ass teachers that be giving us tests every other day.

Oh, I couldn't do that. They're my colleagues.

OK. OK, we can write excuse notes for them explaining why they have to be like that.

Mr. McCourt, the principal is at the door.

My heart sinks.

Into the room the principal escorts the Staten Island Superintendent of Schools, Mr. Martin Wolfson. They don't acknowledge my existence. They don't apologize for interrupting the class. They walk up and down the aisles, peering at student papers. They pick them up for a closer look. Superintendent shows one to the principal. Superintendent frowns and purses his lips. Principal purses his lips. Class understands these are significant and important people. To show loyalty and solidarity they refrain from asking for the pass.

On their way out the principal frowns at me and whispers that the superintendent would like to see me next period even if they have to send someone to cover my class. I know. I know. I've done something wrong again. The shit will hit the fan and I don't know why. There will be a negative letter in my file. You do your best. You take the ball on the hop. You try something that has never ever been done in the whole history of the world. You have your kids hopping with enthusiasm over the excuse notes. But now comes the reckoning, teacher man. Down the hallway to the principal's office.

He is sitting at his desk. The way the superintendent stands still in the middle of the room reminds me of a repentant high school kid.

Ah, Mr. ... Mr ....

McCourt

Come in. Come in. Only a minute. I just want to tell you that that lesson, that project, whatever the hell you were doing in there, was top-notch. Top-notch. That, young man, is what we need, that kind of down-to-earth teaching. Those kids were writing on a college level. He turns to the principal and says, That kid writing an excuse note for Judas. Brilliant. But I have a reservation or two. I'm not sure if the writing of excuse notes for evil or criminal people is justifiable or wise, though on second thought, it's what lawyers do, isn't it? And from what I've seen in your class you might have some promising future attorneys in there. So, I just want to shake your hand and tell you don't be surprised if there's a letter in your file attesting to your energetic and imaginative teaching. Thank you and maybe you should divert them to more remote figures in history. An excuse note for Al Capone is a little risky. Thank you again.

God in heaven. High praise from the Superintendent of Schools in Staten Island. Shall I dance down the hallway or shall I lift and fly?

Will the world object if I sing?

I sing. Next day, I tell the class I know a song they'll like, a tongue-twister of a song, and here it is:

O ro the rattlin' bog, the bog down in the valley O,
O ro the rattlin' bog, the bog down in the valley O.
And in that bog there was a tree, a rare tree, a rattlin' tree,
And the tree in the bog and the bog down in the valley O.

We sang verse after verse and they laughed as they tried to get their tongues around the words and wasn't it great to see that teacher up there singing. Man, school should be like this every day, us writing excuse notes and teachers singing all of a sudden for some reason.

The reason was I realized there was enough material in human history for millions of excuse notes. Sooner or later, everyone needs an excuse. Also, if we sang today we could sing tomorrow and why not? You don't need an excuse for singing.

Photographer David Crosby likes to include a student on his shoots. The day he took Frank McCourt's picture, Crosby's daughter Laurel was his assistant. McCourt, though a little weary, was "immediately interested in Laurel as a student and as a writer. He came alive as a teacher," Crosby said and added, "That evening, McCourt had Hickory rolling in the aisles with his stories about the Catholic Church, growing up in Ireland, and teaching in the Bronx."

155

IRISH POETRY

Billy Collins

That morning under a pale hood of sky
I heard the unambiguous scrape of spackling
against the side of our wickered, penitential house.

The day mirled and clabbered
in the thick, stony light,
and the rooks' feathered narling
astounded the salt waves, the plush arm of coast.

I carried my bucket past the forked
coercion of a tree, up toward
the pious and nictitating preeminence of a school,
hunkered there in its gully of learning.

But only later, as I stood before a wash-stand,
and gaunt, phosphorescent heifers
swam purposefully beyond these windows,
did the whorled and sparky gib of the indefinite
manage to whorl me into knowledge.

Then, I heard the ghost-clink of milk bottle
on the rough threshold
and understood the meadow-bells
that trembled over a nimbus of ragwort—
the whole afternoon lambent, corrugated, puddle-mad.

AFTERLIFE

Billy Collins

Maybe I was waiting at a gate
before flying somewhere
or walking across a pasture toward a cliff,

but I remember thinking
instead of a life directly on the heels of this one,
why not another life running parallel to mine,

a life to sit and watch my first life
though a child's telescope
from a suspicious-looking cloud

a life in which to read everything again
and this time remember every character,
every room, every hidden key and hairpin.

Even a life that took place inside the feedbag
of a livery horse would be better
than just this one followed by the void

I put in my time watching the big stillness
of those horses standing in a line
at the south end of the park,

their oblong heads lowered in the flutter of pigeons.
a raised hoof clomping down on the pavement,
then a blanket placed on the laps of the passengers,

the pull on the reins, and the weight of it all
nodding forward, the tawdry festive harness,
the almost ridiculous white carriage,

and the cruelty or mercy of the driver.
Unless you plan to consort
with hosts of angels or the pandemonium below,

you tell me: would you not risk
the snorting head and big teeth
plunging in if you could have another go?

160

GETTING THE WORDS OUT

(An excerpt from *Self-Consciousness: Memoirs*)

John Updike

The Jerusalem Post of November 10, 1978, having attacked my rumpled attire after I'd lost my luggage,* went on to expose my stutter: "Updike has the slight slurp of a speech impediment, the sort of thing once affected by cavalry subalterns." I liked to imagine, all evidence to the contrary, that it, like my deplorable skin, was unnoticeable—that only I was conscious of it. Conscious, that is, of a kind of windowpane suddenly inserted in front of my face while I was talking, or of an obdurate barrier thrust into my throat. My first memory of the sensation is associated with our Shillington neighbor Eddie Pritchard, a somewhat larger boy than I whom I was trying, on the sidewalk in front of our houses, to reason into submission. I think he was calling me "Ostrich," a nickname I did not think I deserved, and a fear of being misunderstood or mistaken for somebody else has accompanied the impediment ever since. There seems so much about me to explain—all of it subsumable under the heading of "I am not an ostrich"—that when freshly encountering, say, a bored and hurried electrician over the telephone, my voice tends to seize up. If the electrician has already been to the house, the seizing up is less dramatic, and if I encounter not his voice but that of his maternal-sounding secretary, I become quite vocal—indeed, something of a minor virtuoso of the spoken language. For there is no doubt that I have lots of words inside me; but at moments, like rush-hour traffic at the mouth of a tunnel, they jam.

It happens when I feel myself in a false position. My worst recent public collapse, that I can bear to remember, came at a May meeting of the

---

* "Updike is rumpled. Really rumpled. Not the studied casual wrinkles of the well-tenured professor, but crimped-necktie, creased-shirt, battered-jacket, accordion-trousers *rumpled!* Despite the elegant speech, the cocktail cool, the 20 years of New Yorker slick and chic, this man is ragged-assed rumpled! Even his *eyes* are rumpled!" —Byline: Matthew Newvisky

august American Academy and Institute of Arts and Letters, when I tried to read a number of award citations—hedgy and bloated, as citations tend to be—that I had not written. I could scarcely push and better my way through the politic words, and a woman in the audience loudly laughed, as if I were doing an "act." Similarly, many years before, one spring evening, on the stage of the Shillington High School auditorium, I (I, who played the father in our class plays, who was on the debating team, who gave droll "chalk talks" with aplomb even in other county high schools) could barely get out a few formal words in my capacity as class president. I did not, at heart, feel I deserved to be class president (whereas I did somehow deserve to give the chalk talks), and in protest at my false position my vocal apparatus betrayed me. In most people there is a settled place they speak from; in me it remains unsettled, unfinished, provisional. Viewing myself on taped television, I see the repulsive symptoms of an approaching stammer take possession of my face—an electronically rapid flutter of the eyelashes, a distortion of the mouth as of a leather purse being cinched, a terrified hardening of the upper lip, a fatal tensing and lifting of the voice. And through it all a detestable coyness and craven willingness to lease, to assure my talk-show host and his millions of viewers that I am not, appearances to the contrary, an ostrich.

As with my psoriasis, the affliction is perhaps not entirely unfortunate. It makes me think twice about going on stage and appearing in classrooms and at conferences—all that socially approved yet spiritually corrupting public talking that writers of even modest note are asked to do. Being obliging by nature and anxious for social approval, I would never say no if I weren't afraid of stuttering. Also, as I judge from my own reactions, people who talk to easily and comfortably, with too much happy rolling of the vowels and satisfied curling of the lips around grammatical rhythms, rouse distrust in some atavistic, pre-speech part of ourselves; we turn off. Whereas those who stutter win, in the painful pauses of their demonstration that speech isn't entirely natural, a respectful attention, a tender alertness. Words are, we are reassured, precious. The senior Henry James evidently had some trouble enunciating, for after meeting him in 1843 Carlyle wrote to Emerson, "He confirms an observation of mine, which indeed I find is hundreds of years old, that a stammering man is never a worthless one. Physiology can tell you why. It is an excess of delicacy, excess of sensibility to the presence of his fellow-creature, that makes him stammer."

Stuttering is disarming, and may subconsciously be meant to be. Popular culture associates it with fear and overexcitement—"Th-th-there's a t-t-t-tiger in there!"—and of course I was afraid of big blank-faced Eddie Pritchard, afraid of being miscast by him into a role, perhaps for life, that I did not wish to play. I am afraid of the audiences I discomfort and embarrass, to my own embarrassment and discomfiture. I am afraid of New York audiences, especially; they are too smart and left-wing for me. And yet some audiences can be as comforting, with their giant collective sighs and embracing laughter, as an ideal mother—Southern college audiences, particularly; unlike audiences recruited from the tough old Northeast, they hold nary a wiseguy or doubting Thomas or mocking cackle in a thousand, just hosts of attentive and kindly faces shining at the sight of "an author," lightly sweating in their congregation, and drawing forth from my chest my best and true music, the effortless cello throb of eloquence. One could babble on forever, there at the lectern with its little warm lamp, and its pitcher of assuaging water, and its microphone cowled in black sponge and uptilted like the screened face of a miniature fencer. Reading words I have written, giving my own impromptu answers, I have no fear of any basic misapprehension; the audience has voluntarily assembled to view and audit a persona within which I am comfortable. The larger the audience, the better; the larger it is, the simpler its range of responses, and the more teddy-bear-like and unthreatening it grows. But an electrician brusquely answering the phone, or an uniformed guard bristling at the entrance to a building, or a pert stranger at a cocktail party, does not know who I am, and I apparently doubt that my body and manner and voice will explain it. Who I am seems impossibly complicated and unobvious. Some falsity of impersonation, some burden of disguise or deceit forms part of my self, an untrustworthy part that can collapse at awkward or anxious moments into a stutter. The burden was present even in Shillington, perhaps as my strong desire, even as I strove to blend in and recognized each day spent there as a kind of Paradise, eventually to get out.

If fear—fear, that is, of an unpredictable or complex response that might wrench aside my delicately constructed disguise—activates the defect in my speech, then anger, nature's adrenal answer to fear, tends to cancel it. A frontal attack clarifies the mind and stiffens the tongue. Testifying once on my own behalf in a lawsuit, I never thought to stutter; I spoke loudly and carefully, my tone observing no distinction between falsehood and truth. I laid on words as one lays on paint. And I remember with pleasure a reading given long ago, in the fraught and seething Sixties, at some newly founded two-year community college in Dallas, where the audience, instead of presenting the respectful white faces I was accustomed to, consisted of a few young blacks sprinkled in bored postures throughout the arc of plush, mostly empty auditorium seats. It was the Sixties, and black hostility was expected and even to be approved of, and my studiously composed souvenirs of small-town, monarchical life, whether rhymed or unrhymed, did seem rather off the point here; nevertheless, I had contracted to make this appearance, my gorge rose to the challenge, and I gave (in my own ears) one of the better, firmer readings of my negligible public career.

No, it is not confrontation but some wish to avoid it, some hasty wish to please, that betrays my flow of speech. The impediment comes on amid people of whom I am fond, and wish very much to amuse—perhaps to distract them from some fundamental misapprehension that I suspect exists within even our fond relationship. My stuttering feels like an acknowledgment, in conversation, of the framework of unacknowledged complexity that surrounds the simplest exchange of words. This tongue-tripping sense of complexity must go back to my original family, the family of four harried and (except for my grandmother) highly verbal adults into which I was born. As I remember the Shillington house, I was usually down on the floor, drawing or reading, or even under the dining-room table, trying to stay out of harm's way—to disassociate myself from the patterns of conflict, emanating from my mother, that filled the air above my head. Darts of anger rayed from her head like that crown of spikes on the Statue of Liberty; a red "V," during those war years, would appear, with eerie appositeness, in the middle of her forehead. Her anger was aimed rarely at me. I was chastised for coming home late—not so much for being careless or willful about time but for allowing myself to be the weak-minded victim of my retentive playmate. She seemed to fear that I was subject to homosexual seduction, and once scolded me for wrestling with some other boy in the vacant lot across Shilling Alley. On another fraught occasion, her wrath fell heavily on me for cutting my own hair; a forehead lock had kept getting in my way as I bent to a complicated, mirrored tracing toy, and with my paper-cutting scissors I resourcefully snipped it off.

My mother was fanatic about haircuts; the full weight of her underutilized intelligence and sensitivity fell on my head when I returned from the barber's, where each chair was manned, to her fine eye, by a different scissoring style, a different proclivity to error. The prevalent theory about stuttering ties it to parental overcorrection of the three-to-five-year-old child's flawed and fledgling speech. I don't recall every having my speech corrected, but certainly the haircuts with which I returned from Artie Hoyer's barber shop were subject to an overwhelming critique—in detail, behind the ears and at the back of the neck, as well as in regard to overall effect and balance. My mother and I had both been difficult births: a forceps had been used on her, leaving the "V," and my reluctant exit from her womb had left my skull slightly lopsided. Part of the barber's job seemed to be to compensate for this latter irregularity. As my mother looked me over, a hot-house perfectionism enclosed my head and I would hold my breath. My stuttering feels related to the vulnerability of the human head, that odd knob of hair and rubbery moist sensory organs, that tender bud our twig puts out to interact with the air and the psychic waves of others. Other people—their eyes, their desires, their voiced and unvoiced opinions, their harbored secrets—make an atmosphere too oppressively rich, too busy; my sensation, when I stutter, is that I am trying, with the machete of my face, to hack my way through a jungle of other minds' thrusting vines and tendrils. Or, sometimes, it is as if I have, hurrying to the end of my spoken sentence, carefully picked and plotted my way out of a room full of obstacles, and having almost attained (stealthily, cunningly) the door, I trip, calling painful attention to myself and spilling all the beans.

Where these beans have already been partially spilled, the pressure is less. My speech eases where I feel already somewhat known and forgiven, as for example, with:

(1) people from Shillington

(2) people from Ipswich

(3) literary people, especially agents and editors

(4) people who want something from me

(5) women—but not children, at least children whom I have harmed.

With my own children, after I left them, I developed a sharp and painful stutter that had not been there before. I stutter, then, when I am "in the wrong," as, for example, with:

(1) people of evident refinement or distinction

(2) New Englanders of many generations

(3) law-enforcement officers

(4) Israeli journalists and intellectuals

(5) men.

With the second set, my tongue and vocal cords feel caught in some unspo-ken apology for

(1) my psoriasis

(2) my humble origins

(3) my having nothing, as a memorable early review of one of my books put it, to say

(4) my ponderously growing oeuvre, dragging behind me like an ever-heavier tail

(5) my wish to look and live well while simultaneously maintaining an ironical Christian perspective on all earthly gratifications

(6) my voice itself.

The Pennsylvania Germans adapted in various degrees to the dominant English-speaking culture. At one extreme, the Old Order or "house" Amish abjure contemporary dress, the public schools, electricity, and gasoline-powered machinery, and in their church services and social intercourse hold to their dialect of Low German; near the other extreme, the Hoyers were considered especially "English" in their approach. My maternal grandfather spoke a beautiful, cadenced, elocutionary English, though he also would talk to my grandmother in Pennsylvania Dutch. My mother had inherited his silver tongue, and my father came from New Jersey. Thus I was early estranged from the comfortable regional accent of Shillington and Berks County. On my first day at the Ruskin School of Drawing and Fine Art in Oxford, while standing in the enrollment line, I was asked by a fellow American with a strong Southern accent if I were English. I was startled. Had I so thoroughly betrayed my national and regional origins? The legitimacy of my voice, wherever I am, seems a question. In New York and then New England, I have been surrounded by people who do not talk quite as I do. I tend, like a foreigner, to resist dropping consonants (leaving a trace, say, of the "l" in "palm" and elongating "Worcester" as "Woooster" in acknowledgment of the spurned letters; I pronounce words as they look in print, and hence consistently mispronounce "monk," "sponge," and "Wodehouse." Yet we all, in a world of mingling clans, exist in some form of linguistic exile, and most people don't stutter.

So: what to do? As Gerald Jonas pointed out in *Stuttering: The Disorder of Many Theories* (1977), the foremost experts, to a dismaying extent, are inveterate stutterers who still, for all their expertise, can't get the words out. The defect arises, it would seem, from self-consciousness—a failure to let the intricate muscular events of speech be subconscious. Between the thought and the word falls a shadow, a cleavage; stuttering, like suicide and insomnia and stoicism, demonstrates the duality of our existence, the ability of the body and soul to say no to one another. And yet self-consciousness (which does nothing for psoriases but make it agonizing) can be something of a cure here: concentrating on not stuttering, we do stutter less. My flattering father would tell me I had too many thoughts in my head, and that I should speak slower. This did help. Keeping my voice in the lower half of its register also helps; other stutterers, I notice, tend to have high, forced voices, riding a thin hysterical edge. When they manage to speak, it is louder or faster than normal. Stuttering, perhaps, is a kind of recoil at the thrust of your own voice, an expression of alarm and shame at sounding like yourself, at being yourself, at taking up space and air. A well-known principle of speech therapy is that any mechanism which displaces your customary voice—singing, having a sore throat, affecting a funny accent—eliminates the stoppage, the captive tongue is released into Maskenfreiheit, the freedom conferred by masks. The paralysis of stuttering stems from the dead center of one's being, a deep doubt there. Being tired increases the doubt, and—contrary to what one might suppose—so does having had too much to drink; speaking is a physical act and susceptible to the same chemical drags that impair the coordination of other physical acts.

Stuttering, I have come to believe, is a simple matter of breath: we arrive at our ridiculous spasm when in truth we are out of breath, when in our haste and anxiety we have forgotten to breathe. Taking a breath, or concentrating on keeping the breath flowing, erases the problem as easily as mist wiped from a windowpane. Could that have been me, a moment ago, hung up on a mere word? Impossible!

I was intimidated beyond belief to be photographing John Updike. It was rainy and cold outside so we went to the Lenoir-Rhyne alumni house. Updike looked as if he'd just walked off the pages of GQ Magazine. He was a stylish, sophisticated, educated gentleman. In addition, he was generous with his time. (The session lasted 45 minutes.) We talked about golf and his long standing "rivalry" with Joyce Carol Oates. He was enjoying the shoot; enjoying life. And I enjoyed my time with him.

— David Crosby, photographer

THE MYSTERY OF PARENTS

Richard Chess

They become parents in the dark.
Next thing they know

they're a cottage-industry of worry,
agents guarding the nation

of adulthood's secrets.
Eventually, the kids crack

the code: mom's and pop's savings fly away.
Now they've got nothing to call their own.

Still, they might do it again, if they could
remember how, just to be able

to say, in the morning,
do you have your lunch money.

And at three to have a place
to stand, waiting

at the door for the bus to release
a girl or boy or both, imperfect

but right for tomorrow's
clean underwear folded in the drawer.

AWAKE

FOR DEBORAH M^cGILL

Kathryn Stripling Byer

Burning out, the leaves
Cling as long as they can
Before falling. Underfoot
After two weeks of rain

They lie sodden, a slippery carpet
As I walk downhill, wind
Scouring sky to a blue
Finish. What do the dead

Have to teach us? The wisp
Of a last breath? Smoke rising
Out of the ashes? "Walk in
 The world for me," a friend said

Her mother had begged of them,
Sun burning into the earth
Of her last day. I walk down
The hill, watching clouds giving way

So that I can see sun strike the wing
Of a plane disappearing. The river's
Unrolling another day, golden threads
Woven through deep water.

Now, after so many dark mornings,
I walk the world wide awake. Yes, I'm
Minding these leaves underfoot that could bring
Me down. Taking one step at a time.

When we are honest about writing space, esp. if you
are a poet, we take our work wherever we spend a
lot of time, and in my case---it's the kitchen, since I
like to cook. And, well, there's always "work" to be
done there, no matter what.

-- Kathryn Stripling Byer

Wisteria Can't do it

Wisteria

Wisteria "comes back to open the gate?
I had never imagined Wisteria until I
every day soon enough. Trees, flowers, sky,
the predictable present. Wisteria,
wormhole it was into

into what I meant
I had about forgotten
until   again

What will the dead do with their names

Pulled her down to my face
very ago   I knew,
again.   though she was headless of space
and time, I was it was
nothing but air
sidling under the slats of a gate

2 time   could open it I had the
I tried sadley it
type of
phrase: a   mere
dangly of tropes in the same

of mortality soon enough. Don't wash
your brain, she's worth going nowhere
sayin'
so says the lock on the gate.

shrug, somebody
but I can learn. Its too late
to present
I don't care
Pull her down to my face
Unless I let her open the g

others

disturbing rub your

your

FISH

(From *Creatures of Habit: Stories*)

Jill McCorkle

When you learn that you are dying, you take off your glasses and never wear them again. I think that you don't want to see the looks on our faces as we sit here by your bed. I think you want only the blurry outlines of our warm bodies bending and whispering, stroking your face here at the end when they say the senses of touch and hearing are what remain.

The woman who had nursed you when you were a two year old with pneumonia sixty-odd years ago has come to be with you, hold your hand, speak softly about what a fine boy you have always been. We know your story about her and how you've always been sure she was the reason you had survived.

I picture that long-ago scene, you on a little cot in the upstairs hallway, your siblings in the rooms on either side. Two older brothers in one room. Two older sisters in the other. There had been another child, a stillbirth the year before you were born, and there were stories of deformities and how it was a life that was never meant to be. You said that as a child you thought often how your partner had died and worried that you would share his fate, that your life also was never meant to be. When I picture your childhood bed, your little boy face from old photos, the corner of a house 1 remember well though it was torn down a long time ago, I see you, sweaty and shivering, and a young version of this very old woman by your side whispering words of love and kindness.

"Oh honey," she says and then turns away from your bed.

We all know that she can't save you this time.

WHEN THE DOCTOR told you that you were dying, you paused and then said, "I am sixty-four years old and I have had a good life." You have not mentioned death since, except to say that you will be sorry to miss all the events in the lives of your grandchildren: recitals, ball games, graduations, weddings. Jeannie's son, the oldest at eleven, cannot leave your side; he sits and repeats back to you all the stories you began making up for him when he was barely two. We are surprised that he remembers with such detail, but he doesn't want us to listen. It is a secret he shares with you. You have given each of the grandchildren a secret story or joke at some time or another. They all take turns leaning in to kiss you, to whisper, to make you smile. Now you ask that I hold up the baby. "Hold him way up high," you tell me. "I want to see his whole body."

YOU WERE TERRIFIED of the water, but you loved to step into it, chest deep, pool edge within reach. This was your metaphor for life. Nearby I dove, an extension of your limbs. I spiraled and flipped and you held your breath and cheered silently, one hand raised in victory, as I paddled my way back to you.

And we fished, hip deep, waves lapping, surf pulling. You warned me about the undertow, the whirlpools, the stingrays and jellyfish that appeared so benign. And when I caught what we called the toadfish—sharp serrated teeth and spiny jagged gills—you gave up and simply cut the line from the bloody hook wedged too deep within his mouth to reclaim. "Poor old guy," you said as he twisted and flopped against the current. "His girlfriend is going to be so disappointed tonight." You laughed, but I knew from the sadness in your eyes that you understood disappointment better than most.

I asked if he was going to live and you said, "Oh, sure."

"He'll have to stay home from school," you said, nudging me with the pun. "But just think of the fishtales he'll have for his children and grand-children. He will always be the one that got away."

ON YOUR LAST DAY, Mom, Jeannie, and I sit by your bed and sing all of your favorite songs: "When You're Smiling," "I Can't Get Started," "Blue Moon." You stare vacantly upward, your eyes dry and frozen. "Blink," we say.

"If you can hear us, just blink."

WHEN I WENT off to college you offered advice.

1) If you get a flat, do not stop until you can pull into a well-lit, public place. Drive it on the rim if you have to.

2) When you go to a party (if you have to go to a party), fix your own drink (if you have to have a drink). Guard and protect it the whole while just as you do yourself. An unopened beer is always a good choice.

3) You are never too old to come home and it is never too late to call your parents to come and get you.

AND WHEN I needed to come home, you came to get me. Terrified of flying, you flew, white-knuckled, sweaty. And you worried the whole time we loaded everything I owned—not much—and drove out to the interstate in our rental car. We both smoked then and that's what we did all the way home. We played the radio, gave each other an occasional high five or victory sign, and revved our bodies with enough nicotine to go the whole long distance without stopping for the night. The trunk was crammed with things I had owned most of my life—quilts and books, stuffed animals and a rusty three-speed bike that had not worked right since it had gotten stolen and then returned in college. The backseat was filled with forgotten items, some of the wedding gifts still in their original packing—crystal and china and tiny fancy dishes I had never known what to do with. "We all make mistakes," you said every hour or so. "And you're young," you added. "Your whole life is ahead of you."

And now I'm over forty and soon will give your advice to my own children. I have cans of Fix-A-Flat. I have a jack and a spare, flares, thermal blankets, change for a phone call. I always lock my doors. I don't get in a car without glancing into the backseat. I do not go shopping at night by myself, even during the holidays when the parking lots are crowded. I only drink beer in the bottle and I know that I am still not too old to call, just that it's not so easy these days.

I'LL TELL YOU something you might not remember. It was during a summer vacation at Ocean Drive. Remember the little white cottage where we stayed on the bottom floor several years in a row? Young boys sold Krispy Kreme doughnuts door-to-door. Our upstairs neighbor greased his old (you weren't even forty then) body in olive oil and whistled "Red Red Robin" so loud and so often that we all began to exist in that rhythm. There were raft rentals and sno-cones, sand and salt. Jeannie said we should write a note and bury it; she was nine and I was five. She said she had to do the writing. The note said: "It is 1963. We are the Miller sisters. We are two kids from Fulton, who are visiting South Carolina and some day when we are very old, we will return to dig this up and remember the day." She said that when we returned we would drive Cadillac convertibles and live in mansions with handsome husbands. I added that we would have lots of fluffy puppies and kittens and she said she wrote that part down, too, though I couldn't be sure because it was in cursive.

But what I remember most is a can of red Play-Doh and how we had barely arrived and unpacked when I rolled and pressed the clay into the braided rug of the rental cottage. It got stuck there, a sticky mess, and I got in trouble. I rubbed ice cubes over the spot, rubbing and pulling every little speck. And isn't it odd? I knew even as I sat there, rubbing and picking, that I would never forget, that I would think of it often. That I would grow up to believe that rectifying a mistake is sometimes reason enough to exist.

YOUR FATHER MADE his living carving up dead barnyard bodies—cows, lambs, pigs. Your child's eye made no connection between those bloody slabs hanging on hooks and the pet goat you kept in your backyard. You may not have connected the red of your father's eyes to repossessed furniture and your mother's sad anger. You only said nice things and we grew up to love him, so much so that I fell in love with a boy who smelled like him only to later realize that the treasured memory I carried of your father was one of straight bourbon and cigarette gone to ash.

When you were late for school, you told the teacher the goat got loose, that you chased him for blocks on end. This was a teacher you adored, the same teacher who over thirty years later would also teach us, regularly confusing us with Mom, asking with a teasing grin if we were still sweet on you. The goat was your pet. That part was true. But what you really did on those days you hooked school was wander downtown and shoot pool in a dark ancient room where you stood and stared out. Your eyes were always drawn to the light. How frightened you must have been the first time you could not find any light at all. The times your heart was so heavy you could not rise up from the bed. Now if you told your story, others would step forward with their own. Now there are articles and books, more than you could ever read, miraculous "medicines" that take emotionally paralyzed people and bring them back to life. But not then. Then it seemed you were all alone with your fears and worries. And there were many people willing to let you believe that, to believe that your overwhelming sense of loss and sadness made you less of a man. It changed the way that I looked at a lot of people. Though told to respect my elders, I often did not. It was hard to respect ignorance and harder still to respect those who knew better but still offered nothing.

• • •

YOU MUST HAVE seen us standing there those times, children who were afraid to move too far from where you were, even though it was summer beyond the windows of your bedroom and kids from the neighborhood called our names to come out and play tag or hide and go seek, to mount our bikes and take out after the mosquito truck. How shocking it must have been to look down from your hospital window that time and see us there in our Easter dresses waiting for you to come home. We were too young to visit inside, so you came out into the sunlight still wearing a light blue robe and navy terry cloth slippers. You stayed long enough for us to hug and hold onto you while you repeated how sorry you were, sorry that you had to be there. And after you went back inside the tall brick building, one of the adults told me to count up the windows until I got to the fifth floor, that you said you would be there to watch us drive away. I couldn't see you—the windows were caged and dark—but we waved anyway.

You had bought a card for us in the hospital gift shop and we opened it in the car. It was a happy card with ducks and bunnies and chickens, a card about love and joy and the birth of spring. It made us sad. The only resurrection I cared about was yours.

Animals were my closest friends then: cats, dogs—ours, the neighbors', wild skinny strays that I would offer bits of food in hopes of taming. You loved to talk about animals. Your childhood cat, Smoky Mac, once stuck his head in a jar, ears held back in curiosity as his whiskered nose bumped glass. Then he was alert, ears pricked and raised. And he found he could not get loose. He could not get his breath. He ran like wild, heavy jar tight like a helmet, and you, a boy no older than nine or ten, chased after him. You caught his wild body and pinned him down. You cracked the jar with a rock so he could breathe, and though he hissed and scratched, and though he did not come home until the next day, he knew to be grateful. He sat near you whenever he could. He never scratched you or stuck his head in a jar again.

WHEN YOU COME home from the hospital this time, we know that it is the beginning of the end. We know that you will no longer sleep in your own bed, but in one that is equipped with bars and an IV line, an oxygen tube. We will come to rely on the hospice workers who come and go throughout the day.

When you came home that other time, it felt like life was starting again. You were young and had many years ahead of you. There was hope. Your dad arrived in a taxi and sat quietly with his hat on his lap; he wanted to say things but he didn't know how. In less than a year, he would not be able to say anything at all, a stroke and throat cancer having left him to stare out at the end of his life. On one of those afternoons, I went with you to visit him in the hospital, but again, I was not allowed inside. The adults took turns going in so that someone stayed with me under the huge trees where I fed the squirrels, so fat and friendly that they came and sat right in front of me and begged. I asked you to read to me, and you said that you would, but could we please read something other than *The Little Match Girl*. But that was the one I wanted; I wanted to cry. I liked to cry. It had become a kind of hobby, this need to imagine myself or someone I loved taken away. I had to prepare myself. Even now, I feel that's what I'm doing—every word, every image is a match struck in an attempt to hold on.

On the afternoon you die, we keep asking for a sign, a blink, a twitch. We sing "All of Me," "Today," "Moon River." And when it is finally time, Jeannie and I both know at the same moment. We feel it, a static tension in the air, and we communicate it without words, rushing to get Mom to come in from outside where she has finally agreed to go for a rest, rushing to bring your brother to be by your side.

And when you take your last breath, you blink—one strong blink, and then you are gone.

NOW I HAVE DREAMS. One takes place in our old backyard. The swing set casts long-legged shadows toward the house. I pull you up on a swing, tie your arms to the chains to hold you upright. Your head slumps down. You wear the robe of a sick man and I sit beside you, watching and waiting. I am a kid, my hair cropped short, my knees scabbed, my feet bare. My swing creaks back and forth while yours stays perfectly still. And then the people come. A steady stream of strangers passing, looking, nudging, whispering. You are a sick little girl, they say. Sick to sit and hold onto the dead.

But, I say, he's not. He is not dead.

Over and over I argue and then dusk comes and all the people go away. It is almost dark and we are all alone and you lift your head and look at me, your eyes a blue gray I had almost forgotten. You wink. Point your finger and wink. You're right, you say. I am not dead.

YOUR DAD HAD an old collie he called Bruno, a black-and-white creature he walked to the corner store every afternoon. He was retired but he still liked the smell of cold cuts. He liked the way the little market still had a floor covered in sawdust and plenty of bones stashed away for Bruno. This is how I remember your father. Small and neat with a hat he politely tipped at everyone he passed. He held my hand when we crossed the street. His eyes were the same color as yours. This is the man I knew, not the troubled one of your childhood, not the one who stumbled out in front of the bleachers at a high school football game where you sat in the middle of a warm flock of kids, Mom's smooth young hand held firmly in your own. And without a word, you rose to your full height and made your way through the crowd. You never thought to do anything except to carry him home. And if this single act were all I ever knew of you, it would be more than enough.

NOW I DREAM you are in the mirror, bathrobe loosely tied, arms outstretched. I know with the strange knowledge dreams allow that you cannot speak. All the energy you can gather is used to shape your image. And one by one we enter the room. And one by one we ask, Do you see? In the room there are three of us left to mourn and grieve. In the mirror we are a family of four—a simple image of thousands of days. You sign to us with arms reaching, You, and then, hands pressed firmly to your chest, are my heart. Hands crisscrossing, a shake of the head. That's all that there is.

You actually spoke these very words near the end, when your eyes were still able to blink. Tiny tear, cool saliva. "You are my heart; that's all that there is." And on a later day, nearer the end, your eyes dry and frozen in that distant stare, I leaned in close and whispered, "I'll be looking for you."

PART FOUR

WHAT GOES AROUND COMES AROUND
Eleanora E. Tate

"Taneshia, I want a boyfriend for Christmas," said Sudsey. "What do I do?"

"Boyfriend? I don't know," I said. I petted my cat, Rahima, who was lying on the couch by me. "I thought we were supposed to be thinking of ways for me to not have to vacuum the carpet and wash the dishes."

"Come on, Taneshia. You asked me for help getting out of housework. I'm helping you. Now you help me."

"All right, all right. Let me think." I started flipping through the TV channels, but stopped when a lady came on a channel talking about how she could see into the future. "There you go," I said. "Call the psychic hotline."

"Call it for me." Sudsey grabbed my pen off the table and wrote the number on the palm of her hand. "You know Momma won't let me call nobody on TV anymore, not after we ordered those dolls from the Holiday Shopping Network last year."

We had bought two seventy-five dollar Princess Ntombinde dolls with Sudsey's momma's American Express card. I didn't know somebody had to pay real money to American Express later on. When the shopping network wouldn't take back the dolls because we'd cut off the dolls' hair, Momma had to pay Sudsey's mom for my doll. Sudsey's mom paid American Express. Then Momma made me repay her by making me scrub and vacuum our house for a dollar a day. Seventy-five days! I've hated doing housework ever since.

This happened about the same time Momma and Daddy got separated. Now Daddy lived in Michigan, which was a long, long, long way from us in North Carolina. I missed him a lot. I wondered if calling this psychic hotline could help get Momma and Daddy back together again, too.

Sudsey nudged me with her socked toe. "I dare ya two bucks to call."

This is just one part of my work space. The entire work space is much too large to fit into one photo.

185

"Let me think," I said again. I loved to take Sudsey up on a dare, because I usually won. She wasn't as smart as me, even though she was thirteen and in seventh grade. I was eleven. "Where're you gonna find a boy around here not kin to you? Sudsey, if I'm gonna call the psychic hotline you gotta dare me *five* dollars."

"Deal. Now call."

"What boy are you chasing so bad that you're gonna give up five dollars?"

"Roslyn says by fifth grade and absolutely by seventh everybody should have had their first official kiss, by a real boyfriend. I told her I'd had my first kiss, but I haven't. So I gotta get a boyfriend, quick."

"But why do you care what Roslyn thinks?" I asked, frowning.

"Cause Roslyn's popular," Sudsey said, crossing her arms.

"She ain't *that* popular. She's just got a big mouth." That was about the tenth time this afternoon that Sudsey had mentioned her name. Made me sick.

"So call already," she said.

"Okay, but I'm only doing it 'cause we're BFF and you promised about my housework. Do the bump, to make it for real, no backing down." We stood up and bumped each other's right elbows together, then we turned and bumped each other's right hips, then we snapped our fingers three times and did one high five. That was our Best Friends Forever pledge.

But when I called the hotline, I got put on hold. I hated to hold so I hung up. Thank goodness this was a toll-free number, because I got put on hold ten times and never did get through.

"Now you gotta help me," I said. Sudsy told me to only vacuum the middle of the living room floor, so that's all I did. That was a good tip. She brought a dirty spaghetti plate over to Rahima's face. "Lick it," she said, "then I won't have to wash it." Rahima jumped off the couch and walked away stiff-legged.

"Girl, you better wash that plate," I laughed. "I'm not eating on a plate licked by a cat!"

Sudsey stuck the dirty dishes under the sink. She even placed the stinky pot of navy beans that I'd scorched last night down there. I reminded myself to take them out and wash them after dinner tonight. Momma would never know.

I walked Sudsey back down the road to our meeting place by the old house. "Keep calling till you get through," Sudsey said. "When I get the boy you get your money. This is the most important thing in my life." We talked some more under the magnolia tree there, then said good-bye. I hoped nobody ever bought that house because that spot had been our meeting place like forever.

Momma was home when I returned. She sat on the couch with her laptop beside her, looking over some papers. "Hey, big girl, how was school?" she said.

"Same ole thing," I told her.

Momma glanced around the room and smiled a little. "You're doing a good job with cleaning, baby," she said. I thanked her and hoped she didn't see the dust balls by her feet that I'd missed with the vacuum cleaner. When she stood up and walked toward the kitchen, a million brown and white cat hairs floated off her skirt and followed her.

"Sudsey wants to get a boyfriend," I said as I set the table for dinner. "She says she can find out how to do it by calling that psychic hotline. She said Roslyn told her she had to get one so she can get kissed. I think that's stupid."

"I got some advice for her. She doesn't need to call anywhere." Momma took hamburger patties and a package of frozen broccoli out of the refrigerator as she spoke. "Tell her to do her homework and leave the boys alone. Wait a minute!"

Momma turned and stared at me. "Or are you talking about yourself? Boyfriend! You have a hard enough time taking care of Rahima. See how she's rubbing – here, stop! Cat hairs everywhere! And look at these!

Taneshia!"

Momma was opening cupboards and drawers, searching for her red-handled pot. She found it, too, under the sink. "Taneshia Alicia Butler, I'm not even going to ask how these dirty pans and dishes got down here. I'm going to pretend that I hear hot water running and that I see suds flying."

I hauled right over to the sink, twisted on the hot water and started washing quick.

When the telephone rang, Momma answered it. The first thing out of her mouth was, "Taneshia just asked me how to get a boyfriend through that psychic hotline. A boyfriend for *Sudsey*, she *said*. I wasn't born yesterday. Here, Taneshia, talk to Grankie."

Grankie was my grandmother Zanzibar Dorcas. Grankie was my nick-name for her. She lived in a fancy doublewide trailer out in the county. After her daughters – my momma and my Aunt Trippy – got grown, Grankie became an actress and traveled around the world with the Afrika Strutters Theater until Momma and Daddy got separated. Then she retired and came back home to us.

Thanks to Momma, Grankie drilled me for three whole minutes about whether I had a boyfriend, or was trying to get one. "No, Grankie, it's just Sudsy acting silly," I told her.

But that night in bed I listened to my favorite singer Usher on my iPod. I thought about Sudsey wanting a boyfriend. I also began to think about who *I'd* want for a boyfriend. You know, just for make-believe. I fell asleep with Usher singing his heart out, just for me.

Three days after that, just before Thanksgiving, I found a flier stuck in our door. It read: "WANT TO GET THE GUY OF YOUR DREAMS? MOTHER GRATIFY CAN HELP YOU. NO AGE RESTRICTIONS. CALL BETWEEN THE HOURS OF 3-5 PM PACIFIC STANDARD TIME. NO CHARGE TO CALLING PARTY."

I couldn't believe my eyes! I almost squashed Rahima stretching for the telephone. At first I was going to call Sudsey but I decided to call this

Mother Gratify first, just to check her out. I had a heck of a time figuring out what "Pacific standard time" meant, but finally gave up and just dialed.

"Hello, I want to speak to Mother Gratify about getting a boyfriend," I said.

"Oh yes, of course. Just one moment."

By now my heart was pounding like a drum. I told myself to also ask her whether I'd get a laptop for Christmas. And if my folks would get back together again.

A woman with a Spanish accent said hello. "I am Mother Gratify. And you are Taneshia Butler, of course."

"How'd you know who I was?"

"I say what I see," she said.

"Well, I'm calling for my friend. She wants a boyfriend for Christmas."

"Uh-*hunh*. But didn't that flier tell you to call me between three and five P.M. Pacific standard time?"

"I – yeah – but I didn't know what time that was."

"It won't be possible for you to get your friend's wish fulfilled if you can't follow my directions. Anyway, how old is Sudsy?"

"Thirteen – hey, how'd you know her name?"

"Because I say what I see. Isn't Sudsey kind of young to have a boyfriend?"

"I don't know. Miz Gratify, is this going to cost me anything?"

"Not all things are paid for with money. Or credit cards. You happened to be the one thousandth person in this area to call me, so you get three free calls. This is number one."

"I never won anything before." I decided to test her. "Can you tell my horoscope? Do I get a birthday reading? Do you use tarot cards? Do you know my mother or grandmother?"

"So many questions. How can you listen? And if you don't want to listen, you can always hang up so that someone else can call me."

"I'm sorry." She didn't sound mad at me, though. I decided I liked the sound of her voice. It sounded like how warm gingerbread would sound if it could make a noise – spicy.

"You're forgiven," she said. "Now tell me what kind of boyfriend Sudsey wants."

I didn't know about Sudsey but I knew about *me*. "One with lots of money and who drives a red convertible. And he can't have big feet. Who'd like to go to – uh, Busch Gardens in Virginia, and to Mexico, and Bermuda – "

"I thought she wanted one so she could get a kiss. If she wants all that she ought to get a job, save her money, and go with her folks some day."

"But she can't wait that long. She's gotta get him by Christmas." This wasn't going good at all.

"So she needs a rush job. All right. I see a good-looking young man, smart, mannerly, with black hair and deep brown eyes, smooth skin, somebody like, um … who's your favorite singer, Taneshia?"

"Usher."

"Perhaps he looks like this Usher."

"Ohhh yes!" I looked into the telephone's earpiece to see if an eyeball was blinking back at me, because Mother Gratify was peering right into my brain. Wait a minute! I didn't want Sudsey's boyfriend to look like my Usher!

"Miz Mother Gratify, could you, uh, save the Usher-looking boyfriend for – "

"Now, Taneshia, there's a procedure to getting a fellow through Mother Gratify."

My shoulders drooped. I should have known we'd have to pay, no matter what she said. "Well, maybe Sudsey can borrow her – "

"No, Sudsey doesn't need to borrow anything. I told you that payment is not always in money. You must listen to Mother Gratify and follow her directions exactly. Get a pencil, write this down. Number one: Sudsey must clean her room ceiling to floor, wash her curtains, pick up every scrap of paper lying anywhere, vacuum or sweep under her bed and clean out her closet."

"Wait, wait, wait. I'm trying to write this down. Why's she gotta do all that? Is her boyfriend gonna be in her room?" When Mother Gratify remained silent, I figured I better shut up and just write.

"Number two: She must dig the dirt out of the kitchen corners, and wipe out the refrigerator each time anybody spills something in it. Number three: She must wash the dishes, scrub and wax the kitchen floor, and sweep or vacuum the living room and the dining room. That way her boyfriend will see a tidy house where he can sit down. She can offer him some juice or something in a clean glass. Because I understand that Sudsey has twin seven-year-old brothers who like to dirty up stuff."

"But this is a lot of work," I said. I sure was glad I didn't have to do it.

"Now, last. She must dust and sweep and keep her room up every day."

The bump on my finger hurt from so much writing. "Sudsey's gonna croak when she reads this list," I said, grinning. "Anything else?"

"Well, since you initiated this call, and if you want this to work for Sudsey, you have to do the same things."

"Do what same things?"

"Everything you wrote down for Sudsey to do."

"That's not fair!"

"It's the only way Sudsey'll get that boyfriend. Doesn't she help you when you need help? What goes around comes around, you know. You call me back at exactly one P.M. Pacific standard time next Tuesday, one week from today."

"But this is crazy! I can't do all this work!"

"And tell Sudsey to not let you snap at Mother Gratify anymore, either. Good-bye."

I hung up and slumped back on the couch. That lady's words scorched my eardrums so bad they made my face twist up tighter than the rubber bands around my braids. I punched the couch so hard that Rahima sprang away in a cloud of cat hairs.

I dialed Sudsey's telephone number. This darn dare was off!

"So Sudsey, you better bring your fat legs over here and help me do my work, first," I said after I snapped off the work list and Mother Gratify's warning to her. I expected her to have a fit.

All she said was, "Girl, I need that boyfriend bad, and not just to get that kiss. Roslyn's having a Christmas party and she's only inviting couples."

"If you have a boyfriend you can go to her party, but I can't." I frowned.

Sudsey ignored my concern. "Did you tell Mother Gratify what I wanted my boyfriend to look like?"

"Usher" slipped out before I could stop my lips.

Sudsey started to scream. "Shoot yes, I'll clean up my house for him! Usher is too fine! C'mon, you promised to help, so you gotta clean up your house, too. I need this boyfriend double-bad now."

"Then have Roslyn call Mother Gratify for you," I snapped. "Don't forget you still owe me five bucks."

"Hold up, Taneshia. Why you got to act like this? Unless you really want Roslyn to call Mother Gratify for me. I mean, if you can't. Roslyn wants to be best friends with me anyway." She let that hang in the air. Then she added, "And I won't protect you next time when Venita gets mad at you and tries to pull your nose off through the back of your head."

I thought that over, and sighed. "OK, OK. But this ain't right, Sudsey."

"Thanks, girlfriend. I knew you'd come through. I really don't want Roslyn to be my BFF. Her breath smells like a landfill."

For the next two hours I was washing dishes, sweeping the kitchen floor, and even stabbing the kitchen corners with the butter knife to pry out the crud I had let pile up from previous moppings. By the time I finished, my hands were puffy with water blisters, and my back ached. But the kitchen was sparkling clean. I don't think I'd ever cleaned it this thoroughly before. I don't think Momma had, either, not even when Daddy was still here.

When Momma got home, she strolled into the kitchen and – swoosh!

– slid across the slick floor, bumped into me and ended up squashed against me and the refrigerator.

"I waxed the floor," I grunted as we untangled.

"No kidding. Talk about being knocked off my feet!" She glanced around. "Taneshia, I don't know what's got into you, but I sure do love it. The house looks so nice we ought to keep it clean, especially with Thanksgiving this week. Let's go out to eat."

"Oh, good!" We hadn't done that in a long time.

The next afternoon when I telephoned Sudsey she wasn't home, so I vacuumed, then started on my school work. When Momma came home she was so pleased she was grinning from braid to braid.

"You've turned into the Energizer bunny, Taneshia." She slipped her arm around my shoulders. "I know it's been tough for you without your father here, but it's been tough for me, too. We deserve another break. How about a movie?"

"All right!" I hadn't thought much about what it was like for her without Daddy here. They had argued so much she seemed to be glad when he left. Maybe she wasn't after all.

The next day was Thanksgiving. We drove over to Grankie's. I ate so much I felt like a beached whale afterwards. I lay on the couch watching TV while Momma and Grankie played bid whist with Uncle Emery and Aunt Trippy.

Grankie plopped down the ace of spades on Uncle Emery's king and made him and Aunt Trippy lose that hand. "Taneshia, do you know what you want for Christmas?" Aunt Taneshia said as she shuffled cards.

"A Hewlett-Packard laptop, and a Rock Band," I replied. "And clothes, and a cell phone."

"Good gracious, you want the whole store," she laughed. "And how's your friend Sudsey?"

"She's fine."

"With Sudsey in middle school, isn't she kind of old for you to run with?" Aunt Trippy went on. "You know what they say – 'tell me who you hang out with and I'll tell you who you are.' "

"She's only thirteen," I said. Aunt Trippy was so nosy!

"Sudsey's all right." Momma spoke up. "With Taneshia not having an older sister, Sudsey's a big help. They call it BFF – best friends forever, by the way."

"Valesta, if you and your ole man had stayed together Taneshia could be a B-S-F — big *sister* forever — to her own brothers and sisters," Aunt Trippy told Momma. "And what I tried to teach you probably isn't what Sudsey's teaching Taneshia." She arched her eyebrows.

"Well, if you hadn't had your kids so soon Taneshia'd have cousins her age to pal around with now," Momma shot back.

Everybody went, "Uh-oh, look out!" and "Don't go there, Velesta," because Aunt Trippy was only sixteen and eighteen when she had her first children, and they were grown now.

"Trippy, Valesta, quit fussing," Grankie broke in. "Trippy, half the time what you told Valesta didn't make sense. I remember you told Valesta she'd get tapeworms from drinking cow milk. You had her thinking cow milk came from some wild animal and not just regular milk! Taneshia, you help Sudsey, and Sudsey'll help you back. Do good. Don't do bad. What goes around comes around."

"I heard somebody else say that," I told Grankie.

"Who?" she asked. But I just smiled at my secret.

By next Tuesday, Sudsey and I were ready to get our second set of instructions. And we were more than ready to dump all that cleaning. We met at my house and called Mother Gratify at four P.M., after Sudsey figured out the correct time.

"Ask her how old my boyfriend is, where he lives, and what size are his shoes," Sudsey said. She checked her list of questions. "What sports does he like? What's his favorite food, so I can have it in our sparkling clean fridge when he comes over."

Mother Gratify answered on the first ring.

"Let me talk to her," Sudsey yelled.

"No," said Mother Gratify, who heard her. "I can only talk to the person who initiated the call."

"Tell her I did everything you said she said to do," Sudsey ordered. "Ask her what I gotta do next."

"Next we move up to level two," said Mother Gratify. "By the way, ask Sudsey how she feels helping around the house."

When I asked, Sudsey answered, "Tell her I love it," with a wink, but I shook my head no.

Mother Gratify asked how my mother liked my cleaning. "She was happy, 'cause I didn't do it very well before. After Daddy left – they're separated – I didn't want to do it at all." Sudsey nudged me and jerked her thumb at herself. "Sudsy wants to know what else she's got to do."

"All right. A boy likes a smart young lady. How are Sudsey's grades?"

I covered the mouthpiece of the telephone. "Bad news. She said boys like smart girls."

"I'm smart enough. You're the one who can't do fractions. Tell her I get all As."

"I'll accept that," Mother Gratify said when I told her, "even though I'm receiving negative vibrations as to the validity of that response. Next, we must discuss the Courtesy Factor. A boyfriend must have good manners, and he appreciates a young lady who has good manners. Does Sudsy say 'thank you,' 'excuse me,' and 'please'? Does she take baths or showers every day, clean out the tub afterwards, use deodorant, brush her teeth, floss, and so on? And do you?"

"Sure," I said. I knew where this was headed. I hated to clean the tub. "Does this mean – "

"For the next three weeks, until the Tuesday before Christmas, every time Sudsey says something she must say 'please' or 'thank you' or 'excuse me,' whatever's appropriate. That means you do, too, Taneshia."

"But we're through with all that cleaning," I said. "Right?"

"Wrong. You got to keep that up. Call me at this time three weeks from today. That'll be your last call."

"But – "

"I got to say what I see, Taneshia, and I see that young ladies who know how to be tidy, do their homework, make at least Cs, and have good manners get boyfriends like Usher. Or a good substitute."

"But – " I stamped my foot.

"Now you tell me good-bye the way a young lady with good manners does."

"Good-bye, Miz Mother Gratify," I said real low.

I hung up and slapped my hands to my hips. "Sudsey, this is a nightmare. For the next three weeks, we got to say 'thank you' and 'yes ma'am' and 'no ma'am,' 'please,' and everything every time we open our mouths. That's the Courtesy Factor. Plus the housework!"

Sudsey sighed. "This is harder than I thought."

"So are you ready to quit?"

"Nunh-uh. I told everybody at school I had a personal psychic who was getting me a boyfriend like Usher," she said with a big grin.

"But what if it doesn't happen? What if this is just some lady making it up?"

"Then it'll be your fault 'cause you're the one who called her," Sudsey said.

After another week I was ready to drop. I had just enough time after getting home from school to straighten up, do homework, eat, and talk to Momma, take a bath, clean out the tub, and fall into bed with Rahima. But seeing Momma smile at me more made me happy, too. We ate out twice that week, and went Christmas shopping that Friday. I didn't see Sudsey much. When I called her on the telephone, she either only had a few minutes to talk, or she wasn't home. She was running with Roslyn.

Finally the Tuesday before Christmas arrived. Sudsey didn't show up until nearly four-thirty. "Where've you been?" I said, opening the door. "Mother Gratify's gonna be mad at us for not following directions."

Sudsey dragged me outside and pointed to a beat-up red car with blue smoke puffing out the back, sitting in my front yard. A long-necked boy with braids was at the wheel. Beside him sat a girl I recognized as Roslyn. A couple of kids were in the back seat.

"So?" I said, pulling back when I saw Roslyn

"It's him! My boyfriend!" Sudsy whispered. "I mean, almost. He's Roslyn's cousin from Raleigh. He and his folks came down for Christmas. My wish came true! Well, not yet, but I'm working on it. He's fifteen! Were you really doing all that housework? I wasn't. Tell Mother Gratify thanks. Bye!" Sudsey flew across the yard and got into the car.

I opened my mouth to tell her, "Wait!" but I shut it as I watched the car leave. The chilly December wind hit me. I hurried back inside and slumped on the couch. I fought off tears. I felt like an old tin can out rusting in the woods, empty, thrown out, useless.

Sudsey got her wish, and she was BFF with Roslyn. I didn't even get my five dollars. So much for best friends and promises. I decided to call Mother Gratify anyway. But I was sure it was too late for her to help me with my wishes.

When I explained why I was calling so late, Mother Gratify didn't sound upset. "My dear, I'm glad Sudsey got what she wanted. That was the purpose of your calling me in the first place, wasn't it, for your friend?"

"Yeah. But Mother Gratify, Sudsey's hanging around with another girl now, even though I helped her out. And now she's gone and I don't have a best friend anymore."

"Sometimes even friends do stupid things. She's still your best friend. She won't last very long around Roslyn. That boy won't want Sudsey, either. He'll think she's a child. Which she is. Is there anything else you want to ask me?"

"Well, I don't know if you can help me with this, but here goes." I told her how I wished my folks could get back together.

"Mm-hmm. I know that's been bothering you. It'll take a lot more than you doing housework to get them back together," she said. "Remember that it's not your fault they're apart. Things work out the best way they can. I bet your daddy sees you at Christmas. You're such a sweet child. Mother Gratify just loves you. And your grandmomma loves you, too. In fact, I suggest you look out your kitchen window right now. You might be surprised by what you see."

I pulled apart the kitchen curtains and peered outside. I saw Grankie's silver Town Car parked outside our house. Up the road, I saw a long U-Haul truck parked at the old house. "Mother Gratify, excuse me, I got to go. My Grankie's – I mean my grandmother's outside," I said as politely as I could. "Thank you for your advice. I'm glad I got to talk with you. You know what? You're just like my Grankie."

"That's because I *am* your Grankie. Come on out to the car."

"What?" I hung up the telephone and ran outside. "Grankie? How did – "

"Technology's a wonderful thing, isn't it?" said Grankie in a voice that sounded just like Mother Gratify. She held up her cell phone. Before I could say anything, she pointed to a boy about my age walking toward us. He looked just like – just like Usher's brother. Sort of.

He came over to Grankie's side of the car. "Excuse me, lady, we're moving into that house" – he pointed to the old house with the magnolia tree – "and we need to get our electricity turned on. Can my mom use your phone?"

"Let's just come on up and see what we can do," Grankie said.

That boy was talking to Grankie, but you know what? He was smiling right at me.

JOHN McCORMICK

Nikki Giovanni

INVENTORY

Nikki Giovanni

Now that the days are getting shorter
And the nights longer
I stand a bit of bubbly in hand
Observing my home

The roof will make it
I hope
Through the winter
And most certainly the deck
Will not

But there in the corner
An abandoned robin's nest
That wonderful little family that flew
And the heartbreaking one
That threw the egg out

I wish I could have told myself
Why
There must have been some reason they left
But all I had was the loneliness

There in the garden the cilantro continues
To grow
As does the chocolate mint
Two Koi have died
I'm not sure why

And the spiders are coming in

Last year I accidentally swept a large one while
Cleaning the garage then two babies came running and I swept them away too
I have not forgiven myself

And the best part of all this
Is the closing down
And cleaning up and putting away
Hope wraps itself in winter
With the promise
That spring will come

Everything in my home
Is ready for the fierceness of winds
And snows
Ices and below freezing
Temperatures

I do after all
Have you

Mitchell Gold's
New York writing
desk

NICE PEOPLE HAVE NO IDEA
An interview with Mitchell Gold

Mitchell Gold once had the opportunity to interview former U.S. Ambassador Jim Hormel. "We were having," Gold says, "a nice la-dee-dah conversation until I asked him about high school." Hormel, then in his 70s, broke down. He sobbed looking back on his teenage years. He remembered being terrified in boarding school, wanting to be "one of the boys" but knowing he never would be because of the secret he had to keep. Hormel was gay and the risk of public disgrace and expulsion were ever present. "There were," he said, "examples of heterosexual relationships all around me, and the dearth of examples representing what I was feeling underscored its taboo." Asking adults, particularly gay adults, about their struggles in high school opens wounds, wounds that have had decades to heal, but haven't. If gay adults find little or no comfort in recalling their coming of age, imagine the anguish gay teens face while they're in the midst of it?

A handsome man with silver hair and dark eyebrows, Gold wears a black crew neck sweater with jeans for our interview and appears the epitome of comfort but it wasn't always the case. As a boy growing up in New Jersey in the 1960s he was anything but comfortable in his own skin. As he came to terms with the fact he was gay, he was consumed by "a black cloud," unable to ever be fully happy. At first keeping his secret required multi-tasking, but then it escalated to the point where he led two separate lives, one falsely straight, the other gay. By the time he went to college he was an emotional wreck. Fortunately, he asked for help and a psychiatrist led him to accept that being gay was not something that could, or should, be cured. Reaching this realization Gold says was "like being born again" and he reset his course.

To date, his journey has led him to great professional and personal success. In 1989, with Bob Williams, he founded MITCHELL GOLD + BOB WILLIAMS with $60,000 and 23 employees; twenty years later, the company posted sales in excess of $100 million and had more than 700 on its payroll. Gold's spacious office, cozy and quirky at the same time, is decorated with the company's elegant, yet unpretentious, furniture. His desk plays host to organized clutter punctuated by accessories like a giant silver clothespin and touristy snow globes. The company's manifesto begins: *We provide comfort. For everyone.* And ends: *We are on a mission to make the world a more comfortable place.* Even the company's address, One Comfortable Place, underscores the goal. It's a goal Mitchell Gold pursues outside the workplace as well.

Over the years Gold has lent his time and resources to various civil rights organizations. After observing an across the board reluctance to confront religion-based bigotry as the leading barrier to full equality – especially for lesbian, gay, bisexual and transgender individuals – he founded Faith in America. Committed to confronting prejudice and hostility disguised as religious belief, the organization garnered national media attention.

Cox News' Scott Shepard interviewed Gold in 2008 for a piece he was writing on Faith in America. As the two sat in D.C.'s Union Square, Shepard said, "You look like a successful, healthy individual, why spend your resources fighting this battle? You're not suffering..."

"Because," Gold looked down at his feet and said, "I don't want one more kid to go through what I did." He told the reporter of his teenage fears. He talked about his loneliness, depression, his plan to take his own life by age 21 if he were unable to "change"– things he never talked about. Especially with a member of the press.

When Gold finished speaking, Shepard said, tears in his eyes, "I had no idea that's what gay kids go through."

And that was the problem: Nice people had no idea.

It was March, a gorgeous spring day, Gold recalls. "You know, Jefferson Memorial is my favorite, but I looked toward the Capitol. I said, 'That's the answer.' If I could get people's attention there..." He called his sister-in-law Mindy Drucker and asked for help in pulling together a collection of stories about the struggles gay youth endure as they confront their sexual orientation.

Gold sent requests to two dozen people he knew, successful and well-known professionals who'd experienced firsthand what it was like growing up gay. Hoping for fifteen yeses, he planned to call the book *15 at 15*. That title went by the wayside when all but one agreed to participate. One of the first people he contacted, Congressman Barney Frank, the curmudgeonly, powerful, and openly gay Representative from Massachusetts, agreed immediately, saying, "That's brilliant! This is just what this country needs." In his piece, Frank recalled the political climate during the Eisenhower years, when at age 13 he was coming to grips with his sexuality: "...gay or lesbian[s] were unworthy of serving our own federal government because our alleged degenerate moral character and susceptibility to blackmail made us security risks." Frank related how, to safeguard his political career, his own coming out happened "in three stages." Most importantly, he wrote that in today's Washington, so different than Eisenhower's, being open about his private life has actually helped his career, and has allowed him to fight prejudice against gays from a prominent, national platform.

Then word got out and others wanted to be part of the project – people such as Bishop Gene Robinson and actor Richard Chamberlain. The project grew to include more than three dozen stories; *40 at 15* didn't have the same ring and Gold conceived a new title, *CRISIS: 40 Stories Revealing the Personal, Social and Religious Pain and Trauma of Growing Up Gay In America*.

In some cases, Gold and Drucker interviewed contributors, in other cases they edited the pieces as they came in. In initial drafts, many avoided digging beneath the surface and Gold had to probe for the real story. He recalls working with Hilary Rosen, former CEO of the Recording Industry Association of America. "Her story was okay," Gold says. "Everything was fine. She came out in college. But I asked her, 'Why not in high school?' I said,

'Tell me the day before you told your mother.'"

Rosen told him she panicked. She feared if she came out she'd never reach her career goals. And they were lofty goals. "I had it all figured out," she says. "I would become CEO of a Fortune 500 company but participate in politics enough so that I would be appointed to a vacancy in the U.S. Senate." Coming out put those dreams in jeopardy. "I was in a crisis," she said.

Crisis is indeed the watchword; the book is full of stories about critical turning points in the lives of gays. Sometimes coming out means the end of family life, or the end of a career, or ultimately, in some cases, the end of a life.

Gold says the most interesting thing about writing this or any book, is that it's far more work than one might anticipate. While he found it particularly exhausting to collect the forty stories in *CRISIS*, he realized early on that interviewing and editing were only the tip of the iceberg. He would need to do additional research and become an expert on the subject. His fact-finding brought him face to face with alarming statistics, statistics he hates to share.

- *Gay youth, rather than express anger toward a tormentor, internalize their emotions and take their anger out on themselves, emotionally and sometimes physically.*
- *Gay teens are at substantially higher risk of dropping out of school (28%, three times the rate of heterosexual students).*
- *They are more likely to be kicked out of their homes and turn to life on the streets.*
- *Gay teens are four times more likely to commit suicide than their heterosexual peers.*

Faith in America published 20 thousand copies of *CRISIS* and in the fall of 2008 the book debuted in major metropolitan centers recognizable solely by their initials: NYC, LA, DC. The launch events (30 in two months) drew huge crowds, with many celebrities in attendance. It wasn't long until *CRISIS* generated some interest in Gold's own backyard.

Rand Brandes, Lenoir-Rhyne University's Martin Luther Stevens Professor of English and director of the school's Visiting Writers' Series, asked him to be one of the featured writers for the 2009-2010 season.

The Lenoir-Rhyne student body includes a high number of education majors and Gold was excited by the opportunity to talk to future teachers. He wanted them to learn about the silent epidemic of depression, isolation and fear rampant among gay youth and what they – especially as teachers – could do to stop it. Given that the University is in Hickory, NC, the majority of this audience was not likely to be as receptive to the stories in Gold's book as their urban counterparts. But Gold believed the Hickory community needed to hear accounts from grieving parents who have lost gay children to suicide. And they especially needed to know the role the church plays in perpetuating bullying, bigotry and prejudice. He wanted them to hear about Jarod K. from Texas who cut himself because he did not know how to handle being gay, and who, after asking his minister for help, was encouraged to cut himself more to "get the demons out."

Though the question of sin had not been paramount for Gold when he began *CRISIS*, ensuing interviews revealed it to be the biggest issue for many gay youth today. "I had to touch that," he said. "We have to get being gay off the 'Sin List.'" To do that ministers had to be engaged in the conversation and what better place to do that than in the Bible Belt?

Gold remembers once being in an audience while a former minister talked to children and their parents about his being gay. "It may be how you're born," the minister conceded, "but you can control your behavior." The minister could not sanction loving relationships between gay couples, even for himself! It was the familiar, "Love the sinner, hate the sin" rhetoric. To Gold's way of thinking, pastors who preach this kind of message are nothing less than emotional child molesters. Worse, they enable abusive and discriminatory behavior in their congregations.

Dan Karslake titled his introductory piece in *CRISIS*: "Could You Live With Being Called an Abomination?" Self-hatred is one difficult issue to overcome, but to make gay kids believe God hates them, too, Karslake believes is nothing short of criminal. Words of judgment and condemnation from too many pulpits have pushed too many gays to take their own lives. Karslake relates some interesting truths. "The Bible says absolutely nothing about homosexuality as we know and understand it today," he writes. "In fact, the word *homosexual* didn't even appear in any Bible in any language until 1946!"

Too often, religious-based teachings violate others' civil rights. When Gold speaks in rural settings about the stories in *CRISIS*, well-meaning, hard-working Christians want to know how not to hate their sons, daughters, friends when they are gay. He laments, "Though Martin Luther King, Jr. accomplished many things, he did not break the back of religion-based bigotry." Gold uses the expression, "the keys to the Kingdom," and to him that means getting the conversation of religious teaching on the table. Gold was encouraged by a poll that showed 51% of Southern Baptists now believe being gay is not a sin. To him that means progress. But there is still a long way to go and that is one reason why he accepted Lenoir-Rhyne's invitation.

Rather than structuring the event around a typical lecture-based presentation, Brandes suggested more of a discussion format. "Why don't you get one of your fancy friends to interview you?" he asked, half-joking. Considering the circles Gold moves in, this wasn't such a far-fetched notion.

Tipper Gore, wife of former Vice President Al Gore, couldn't fit the date in her schedule, but CNN anchor and special correspondent Soledad O'Brien could.

Gold and the University worked hard to get an audience, placing ads in all the local papers, even in outlying rural areas such as Valdese and Taylorsville. They sent letters to every Hickory area church and Gold says, "There not there are not many gay-affirming churches around here." They even placed some television ads.

Their efforts paid off. The night of January 28, 2010, P.E. Monroe Auditorium on the Lenoir-Rhyne campus was packed with more than 1000 community members and students.

Center stage sat two creamy yellow armchairs; between them a copper tray balanced on an upholstered footstool. Behind, stood a row of bookcases. Two end tables with matching lamps framed the warm and inviting setting.

O'Brien, stage right, her hair in a ponytail, wore a patterned jacket paired with a black skirt and black boots. Gold sat opposite her, dressed in a black suit and white shirt. (He avoids ties as a rule, preferring to appear more approachable and this night was no exception.) After some lighting and sound checks, the interview began. Both appeared at home – comfortable and at ease with one another and with the topic they were there to discuss.

Did he have the questions in advance? "Trust me when I tell you," he smiles and emphatically shakes his head no. Earlier that day Gold met O'Brien at the airport and on the drive to Hickory they scarcely mentioned the book. Gold did try to get at least a hint of what she had planned. "I told her, 'You know I have very little experience with this sort of thing and it would be helpful if I just knew the first question, so I don't get thrown for a loop.'"

No dice. "I haven't thought of it yet," she said. And even though, prior to the interview, she stayed at Gold's house, he swears the first time he heard her questions was when the audience heard them.

One question in particular stands out for Gold. "Soledad asked what I wanted to accomplish with creating this book. I can't remember being asked that simple question before. I answered that I hoped people would be inspired to stop being complicit with the harm. ...to challenge their clergy...to challenge those at the water cooler who make disparaging remarks. As I spoke I could sense virtually all in the audience nodding their heads in agreement."

Gold and Brent Childers, a former journalist and lifelong conservative evangelical Christian and now Executive Director of Faith in America, chose a few excerpts to be read from *CRISIS* following the interview portion of the evening. They asked a Lenoir-Rhyne student to read from a young person's chapter and Childers read about his own progression from believing homosexuality is a sin to understanding how false and hurtful such church-based teachings are.

Being onstage at Lenoir-Rhyne University was very different than the *CRISIS* launch events. "In a metropolitan area, I'm more focused on getting people to not be so apathetic," Gold says. Apathy allows, however unwittingly, harm to continue. He says the difference in Hickory was that he wanted to change hearts and minds. No matter where he speaks, the reality is that people have a hard time talking about sex and religion. "I do my best to create an environment where people will speak more freely."

His skill at doing so was especially evident during the Q&A period following the interview. The first audience member to ask a question called on Gold "to receive Christ as your personal savior." This comment came as no surprise. He says people often try to save his soul. "They'll say, 'Mitchell, what do you think about Jesus?' and I say quite honestly, 'I wish he were here right now.'" That night, when a particularly vocal evangelical minister fired a barrage of questions, Gold says eventually he "just got really tired." When the pastor began to speak in circles, Gold "didn't want to embarrass him any more" and brought closure to the exchange.

Gold credits Childers for helping him develop a calm and constructive demeanor when faced with this kind of opposition. As recently as 2003, Childers was an ardent follower of the Religious Right and had publicly derided gay and lesbians under the banner of Christianity. Gold says, "He knows what people are thinking as he's thought those things before in his past life."

Gold also has benefitted from media training with Bishop Gene Robinson, the country's first openly gay Episcopal bishop. Robinson says he tries to "bring joy" to the room as soon as he walks in and he stays centered on that. This advice resonated with Gold. "I recognize that there are so many well meaning people who just don't understand the harm they are causing others." He's seen that he can change far more attitudes with "kind education" than with ranting and raving.

"This is a volatile issue – even when it's not really about sex," Gold says. "My goal all along has been to get people talking." The more people actually talk about this issue, the more they see it doesn't make sense to be on opposing sides.

Since that evening at Lenoir-Rhyne, there has been a decided change in the community. Many have stepped up and, in Gold's words, "have stopped being complicit." The interview that took place on those comfortable yellow chairs in the P.E. Monroe Auditorium was a catalyst for many conversations. Brandes believes it was the first public conversation about the issue ever held on the Lenoir-Rhyne campus. He goes so far as to say it was "a cultural turning point at Lenoir-Rhyne and for Hickory." The editor of The Hickory Daily Record told Gold afterward that his brother is gay and now he intends to step forward and be more supportive. Gold has since been invited to speak at other Hickory venues and has sat down to lunch with the pastor who peppered him with questions that January night. Gold holds out hope for the minister who now professes on his blog that he is "trying to learn." And that is a start.

This Visiting Writers' Series event stands apart. It did not feature a literary luminary, a prophetic poet, or a best-selling author. It was not about entertainment. "This was important," Gold says. "It was about understanding and that's what education is all about."

—*Avery Caswell*

WHAT THOU LOVEST WELL

Sharon Olds

(Ezra Pound, Canto 81, *Pisan Cantos*)

And then, in the night, I wake up, and I can't
remember how I met my ex,
and I think: I let a stranger into
my life. Then I remember we met at a party,
he was the friend of a friend of a friend — all
medical students, which seemed, to me,
those days, as if they were bonded and insured.
But I did not know him. Suddenly I understand that my parents were strangers to me —
like a pair off the street, I took them in,
in a wave of alchemy, to the cells
of my body and brain, I gave them fresh being,
I did not know who they were, and when they
showed me who they were, I did not believe it,
I would not know them, I kept them strangers,
I would not see them — and my chosen mate,
I could not, or would not, know him, and we
cannot love what we do not know, or we
cannot love it well enough. "What thou
lovest *well* remains, the rest is dross;
what thou lov'st well cannot be reft from thee,
what thou lov'st well is thy true heritage."

INTERACTIVE CHALLENGE:
match the desk with the writer

mark
powell

1.

donald
secreast

2.

bret
lott

3.

richard
chess

4.

GOODBYE TO THE SUNSET MAN

Lee Smith

Once again my husband and I line up for sunset cruise tickets on the tall vintage schooner Western Union, which sways in its dock here at the end of William Street, here at the end of America.

"How many?" The handsome blonde in the ticket booth looks like she used to be a man.

"Three," I say.

"Two," Hal says, turning around to look at me.

"So how many is it?" She drums her long nails on the wooden counter.

"Two," Hal says. He gives her his credit card.

She slides over two tickets for the sunset cruise and two coupons for free drinks, which we order on the roof of the Schooner Wharf Bar where we wait until time to board. This year we are here without my son, Josh, who died in his sleep this past Oct. 26. The cause of his death was an "acute myocardiopathy," the collapse of an enlarged heart brought about, in part, I believe, by all the weight he had gained while taking an antipsychotic drug. He was 33; he had been sick for half his life, doing daily heroic battle with the brain disorder that first struck while he was in a program for gifted teen musicians at the Berklee College of Music in Boston, the summer between his junior and senior years in high school.

Back in Chapel Hill, we'd started getting wilder and wilder phone calls from him about "birds flying too close to the sun," reports of all-night practice sessions on the piano, strange encounters in the park, and no sleep—no sleep, ever. He flew home in a straight jacket.

Then the hospitalizations began—first a lengthy stay at Holly Hill in Raleigh followed by a short, heart-breaking try at returning home to normalcy and Chapel Hill High; then longterm care at Highland Hospital in Asheville, where he lived for the next four years, sometimes in the hospital itself, sometimes in their group home, sometimes in an apartment with participation in their day program. For a while he was better, then not. All kinds of fantasies and scenarios rolled through his head. He moved, talked and dressed bizarrely; he couldn't remember anything; he couldn't even read. We brought him back to UNC Neurosciences Hospital. They referred him to Dorothea Dix's test program for the new "wonder drug" clozapine, just legalized in this country (1992).

Up on that beautiful, windy hill looking out over the city of Raleigh, Josh started getting truly better for the first time. He could participate in a real conversation; he could make a joke. It was literally a miracle.

He was able to leave the hospital and enter Caramore Community in Chapel Hill, which offered vocational rehabilitation, a group home and then a supervised apartment—as well as a lot of camaraderie. He came in with some great stories as he worked with the Caramore lawn and housecleaning business ... my favorite being the time the housecleaning crew dared one of the gang to jump into the baptismal pool at a local church they were cleaning—and then they all "baptized" him on the spot. Before long he graduated into a real job at Carolina Cleaners. Against all odds, Josh had become a "working man," as he always referred to himself; his pride in this was enormous.

Though other hospitalizations ("tune-ups," he called them) would be required from time to time, Josh was on his way. He lived in his own apartment, drove a car, managed his weekly doctor visits, blood tests, pharmacy trips and medication. But as the most important part of his own "treatment team," he steadfastly refused his doctor's eventual urging to switch to one of the newer drugs, such as olanzapine, risperidol or geodon, in hopes of jump-starting his metabolism. Clozapine had given him back his life, and he didn't want to give it up. And in spite of his weight and smoking, he seemed healthy enough; physical examinations didn't ring any warning bells.

Josh became a familiar figure in Chapel Hill and Carrboro, with friends and acquaintances all over town—especially his regular haunts such as Weaver Street and Caffe Driade, where he went every day. Josh worked at Akai Hana Japanese Restaurant in Carrboro for the last seven years of his life, doing everything from washing dishes to prep work to lunchtime sushi chef. He was the first one there every morning—he opened up and started preparing the rice. It was his favorite time of the day, as he often said. He played piano at Akai Hana every Saturday night: a mix of jazz, blues and his own compositions.

The live music produced by the Wharf Bar's Jimmy Buffet wannabe band is way too loud, and our drinks, when they come, are a startling shade of red, with umbrellas in them. Hal raises his plastic glass high. "Here's to the big guy," he says. We drain them.

Josh considered the schooner trip a requisite for his annual Key West experience. He loved the ritual of it all, beginning when the crew invited the evening's passengers to participate in raising the mainsail. He always went over to line up and pull, passing the halyard hand over hand to the next guy. He loved to stand at the rail as we passed the town dock and Mallory Square, where all the weird pageantry of the sunset was already in full swing: the tourists, the guy with the trained housecats, the flame swallower, the escape artist tied up in chains, the oddly terrifying cookie lady. The aging hippie musician on board invariably cranked up "Sloop John Bee" as we headed out to sea while the sun sank lower on the starboard side. The sun was so bright that I couldn't even face it without sunglasses, but Josh never wore them. He just sat there perfectly still, staring straight into the sun, a little smile playing around his lips.

What thoughts went through his head on that last voyage?

Perhaps more to the point, what thoughts did not go through his head, in this later stage of schizophrenia characterized by "blank mind" and "lack of affect?" Gone the voices, gone the visions, gone the colored lights, to be replaced by ... what? Maybe nothing, like the bodhisattva, a person who has achieved the final apotheosis, beyond desire and self. Here he sat, an immense man in a black T-shirt and blue jeans, silent, calm, apparently at peace. He no longer seemed to know what he had lost. Some call this a "blessing," and some days I am among them; but most days I am not, remembering instead that wild boy of 17 who wanted the world—all the music; all the friends, BMX bikes and skateboards; all the poetry; all the girls—all the life there ever was.

Now the captain is blowing the conch shell from the deck of the Western Union. We stand. The sun slants into our eyes. A breeze is coming up. I pull on my windbreaker, fingering the little bronze vial of ashes in my pocket.

It's time.

Last January (2003) Josh and I flew into Key West together, arriving late on a cool and blustery Tuesday night around 9 p.m. Wind rattled the palm fronds as we walked out onto the brightly lit but somehow lonely looking Duval Street. Only a few people scurried past, their shoulders hunched against the wind. We passed the funky Chicken Store, a "safe house" for the much-maligned chickens that have overrun Key West. We passed the Scrub Club, an "adult" bathhouse that usually featured its scantily clad ladies blowing bubbles over the balcony rail, calling out, "Hi there! Feeling dirty? Need a bath?" to the amused passersby. But it was too cool for bubbles that night, and the girls were all inside behind their red door. The wind whipped paper trash along the street.

We crossed Duval and went into the friendly looking Coffee and Tea House, where big trees overhung an old bungalow with a porch and yard filled with comfortable, mismatched furniture. Josh was very tired. He had that out-of-it, blank look he sometimes gets, almost vegetative, like a big sweet potato. We walked up the concrete steps and into the bar with its comforting, helpful smell of coffee brewing. People clustered at little tables, on sofas, in armchairs in adjacent rooms, talking and reading the newspapers strewn everyplace.

The bartender's long, gray hair was pulled back into a ponytail. He came over to Josh and said, "What can I get for you, sir?"

"Well, I'll tell you," Josh said in a surprisingly loud voice (maybe it even surprised him), shaking his head like a dog coming up from under the water. "I'll tell you, buddy, I don't know what the hell it is I want, and I don't know where the hell it is I am, and I don't know what the hell it is I'm doing!"

Heads along the bar swiveled, and the bartender burst out laughing. "In that case, sir, you've come to the right island!" he announced, as everybody applauded.

Josh had found his Key West home for the next week. At bars or beaches, he talked to everybody; you never knew what he was going to say next.

He told a great version of the Christmas story, too, conflating the Bible with O. Henry: "Once upon a time there was a young girl who was very sick, and somehow she got the idea that she would die when all the leaves fell off the tree that grew just outside her bedroom window. One by one they dropped. She got sicker and sicker. Finally there was only one red leaf left on the tree; she was just about to die. That night while she was asleep, Jesus flew up to her window. Jesus was a French artist. He wore a red beret. So he brought his box of oil paints with him and painted red leaves all over the window, finishing just as the sun came up and the last red leaf fluttered down to the ground. Then he flew away. Then she woke up, and she was well, and it was Christmas."

Answering the question of whether or not he believed in Jesus, he said, "Well, I don't know. Every time I'm in the hospital, there are at least three people in there who think they're Jesus. So sometimes I think, well, maybe Jesus wasn't Jesus at all—maybe he was just the first schizophrenic."

Josh's eventual diagnosis was schizo-affective, meaning partly schizo-phrenic (his mind did not work logically, his senses were often unreliable, his grip on reality sometimes tenuous) and partly bipolar—actually a blessing, since the characteristic "ups and downs" allowed him more expression and empathy. But diagnosis is tricky at best. The sudden onset of these major brain disorders usually occurs in the late teens or early twenties, and it's usually severe. But all psychosis looks alike at first. There's no way to distinguish between the "highs" of bipolar illness, for instance, and the florid stage of schizophrenia—or even a garden variety LSD psychosis. Reality had fled in every case. The best doctors make no claims; "Wait and see," they say.

As far as prognosis goes, medical folklore holds to a "rule of three": About a third of all people with major psychotic episodes will actually get well, such as Kurt Vonnegut's son, Mark, now a physician who wrote the memoir *Eden Express*. The next, larger group will be in and out of hospitals and programs for the rest of their lives, with wildly varying degrees of success in work and life situations; the final group will have recalcitrant, persistent illnesses which may require lifelong care or hospitalization—though now, I suspect, the new drugs and community care models have shrunk this group considerably.

But here's the bottom line: All mental illnesses are treatable. Often, brain chemistry has to be adjusted with medication. If symptoms occur, go to the doctor. Don't downplay it, don't hide it—seek treatment immediately. Mental illness is no more embarrassing than diabetes. And the earlier we get treatment, the more effective it will be. I myself could never have made it through this past year of grief and depression without both counseling and medication. We are also lucky to have organizations and support groups in this area to help us and our families cope. As Josh proved, very real, valid and full lives can be lived within these illnesses.

Now my husband and I sit discreetly at the very back of the Western Union, right behind the captain at the wheel. He has given the order; the crew has cried "fire in the hole" and shot off the cannon. We have covered our ears. We have gotten our complimentary wine, our conch chowder. We have listened to our shipmates talk about how much snow they left behind in Cleveland, how many grandchildren they have, and how one guy played hockey for Hopkins on that great team in 1965. Then we duck as, with a great whoosh of the jib, we come about. We sit quietly, holding hands, hard. Now there's a lot of wind. All around us, people are putting on their jackets.

Independent of any of this, the sky puts on its big show, gearing up for sunset. The sun speeds up as it sinks lower and lower. The water turns into a sheet of silver, like a mirror.

Like Hal, Josh was a major sunset man, always looking for that legendary green flash right after the sunset, which nobody I know has ever actually seen, though everybody claims to have known somebody who has seen it. Here where sunset is a religion, we never miss the moment. In Key West the sun grows huge and spreads out when it touches the water, so that it's no longer round at all but a glowing red beehive shape that plunges down abruptly to the thunderous applause of the revelers back at Mallory Square.

"Get ready," Hal says in my ear. "But look, there's a cloud bank, it's not going to go all the way."

I twist the top of the vial in my windbreaker pocket.

The sun glows neon red, cut off at the bottom by clouds.

A hush falls over the whole crowd on board the Western Union. Everybody faces west. Cameras are raised. It is happening.

"Bon voyage," Hal says. Suddenly, the sun is gone. The crowd cheers. I throw the ashes out on the water behind us; like a puff of smoke, they disappear immediately into the wake. I say, "Goodbye, baby." Nobody notices. The water turns into mother of pearl, shining pink all the way from our schooner to the horizon. The scalloped edge of the puffy clouds goes from pink to gold. The crowd goes "aah." *Goodbye baby*. But no green flash. The crowd stretches, they move, they mill around on deck. The light fades and stars come out.

I don't agree with the theory that mental illness conveys certain gifts. Even if this sometimes seems to be the case, as in bipolar disorder's frequent association with creativity, those gifts are not worth the pain and devastating losses the illness also brings with it. Yet sometimes there are moments....

I am remembering one starry summer night back in North Carolina, the kind of breathtakingly beautiful summer night of all our dreams, when Josh and I took a long walk around our village. He'd been staying with us for several days because he was too sick to stay in his own apartment. He'd been deteriorating for months, and his doctor had arranged his admission to UNC's Neurosciences Hospital for the next morning. Josh didn't know this yet. But he was always "compliant," as they call it. We were very lucky in this. My friend's son wouldn't take his medicine and chose to live on the street; she never knew where he was. Schizophrenia is like an umbrella diagnosis covering a whole crowd of very different illnesses; but very few people with brain disorders actually become violent, despite the stereotype.

Josh liked the hospital. It was safe, and the world he'd been in that week in North Carolina was not safe, not at all, a world where strangers were talking about him and people he used to know inhabited other people's bodies and tables turned into spiders and all the familiar landmarks disappeared so that he couldn't find his way anywhere. He couldn't sleep, he couldn't drive, he couldn't think.

Yet on that summer night in Hillsborough, a wonderful thing happened. We were walking through the alley between the old Confederate cemetery and our back yard when we ran into our neighbor Allan.

"Hi there, Josh," Allan said.

Instead of replying, Josh sang out a single note of music.

"A flat," he said. It hung in the hot honeysuckle air.

"Nice," Allan said, passing on.

The alley ended at Tryon Street, where we stepped onto the sidewalk. A young girl hurried past.

"C sharp," Josh said, then sang it out.

The girl looked at him before she disappeared into the Presbyterian Church.

We crossed the street and walked past the young policemen getting out of his car in front of the police station.

"Middle C," Josh said, humming.

Since it was one of Hillsborough's "Last Friday" street fairs, we ran into more and more people as we headed toward the center of town. For each one, Josh had a musical note—or a chord, for a pair or a group.

"What's up?" I finally asked.

"Well, you know I have perfect pitch," he said—I nodded, though he did not—"and everybody we see has a special musical note, and I can hear every one." He broke off to sing a high chord for a couple of young teen girls, then dropped into a lower register for a retired couple eating ice cream cones.

"Hello," another neighbor said, smiling when Josh hummed back at him.

So it went all over town. Even some of the buildings had notes, apparently: the old Masonic Hall, the courthouse, the corner bar. Josh was singing his heart out. And almost—almost—it was a song, the symphony of Hillsborough. We were both exhilarated. We walked and walked. By the time we got back home, he was exhausted. Finally he slept. The next day, he went into the hospital.

Josh loved James Taylor, especially his song "Fire and Rain." But we were too conservative, or chickenshit, or something, to put it on his tombstone, the same way we were "not cool enough," as Josh put it, to walk down the aisle to "Purple Rain" (his idea) while he played the piano on the day we got married in 1985.

But now I say the words to Hal as the light fades slowly on the water behind us.

I've seen fire and I've seen rain
I've seen sunny days that I thought would never end
I've seen lonely times when I could not find a friend
But I always thought that I'd see you again.

Well, I won't. I know this. But what a privilege it was to live on this earth with him, what a privilege it was to be his mother. There will be a lessening of pain, there will be consolations, I can tell. But as C.S. Lewis wrote in *On Grief*: "Reality never repeats... . That is what we should all like, the happy past restored"... as it can never be, and maybe never was. Who's got perfect pitch, anyway? Yet to have children—or simply to experience great love for any person at all—is to throw yourself wide open to the possibility of pain at any moment. But I would not choose otherwise. Not now, not ever. Like every parent with a disabled child, my greatest fear used to be that I would die first. "I can't die," I always said whenever any risky undertaking was proposed. So now I can die. But I don't want to. Instead, I want to live as hard as I can, burning up the days in honor of his sweet, hard life.

Night falls on the schooner ride back to Key West. I clutch the bronze vial that held some of Josh's ashes, tracing its engraved design with my finger. The wind blows my hair. The young couple in front of us are making out.

"Let's get some oysters at Alonzo's," Hal says, and suddenly I realize that I'm starving.

"Look," the captain says, pointing up. "Venus."

Sure enough. Then we see the Big Dipper, Orion, Mars. Where's that French artist with the red beret? No sign of him, and no green flash, either—but stars. A whole sky full of them by the time we slide into the dock at the end of William Street.

APPROACHING A SIGNIFICANT BIRTHDAY, HE PERUSES

THE NORTON ANTHOLOGY OF POETRY

R. S. Gwynn

All human things are subject to decay.
Beauty is momentary in the mind.
The curfew tolls the knell of parting day.
If Winter comes, can Spring be far behind?

Forlorn! the very word is like a bell
And somewhat of a sad perplexity.
Here, take my picture, though I bid farewell,
In a dark time the eye begins to see

The woods decay, the woods decay and fall–
Bare ruined choirs where late the sweet birds sang.
What but design of darkness to appall?
An aged man is but a paltry thing.

If I should die, think only this of me:
Crass casualty obstructs the sun and rain
When I have fears that I may cease to be,
To cease upon the midnight with no pain

And hear the spectral singing of the moon
And strictly meditate the thankless muse.
The world is too much with us, late and soon.
It gathers to a greatness, like the ooze.

Do not go gentle into that good night.
Fame is no plant that grows on mortal soil.
Again he raised the jug up to the light:
Old age hath yet his honor and his toil.

Downward to darkness on extended wings,
Break, break, break, on thy cold gray stones, O sea,
And tell sad stories of the death of kings.
I do not think that they will sing to me.

228

WRITING WITH SO GREAT A CLOUD OF WITNESSES

Bret Lott

1

Last month my best friend, Jeff Deal, and I made a road trip from Charleston, South Carolina, to Fort Campbell, Kentucky, to visit my older son Zebulun, a Cavalry Scout with the 101st Airborne. Jeff's son Russell is in the Army as well, our two boys having made a pact while they were undergrads at Furman University that they would finish college, take a year off, and then join up in order to serve their country in return for the blessing of freedom we have been given and too often take for granted. Both our boys have served their tours of duty in Iraq and come home safely, and now Zeb would be getting married in two weeks. I wanted to surprise him, spend some time with him alone, and just be father and son one last time before all in his life changed. And because Jeff, too, is a father who knows what it is to love and miss and pray and worry over a son, he joined me for the eleven-hour drive up to Kentucky and back.

Our families have been friends for over twenty years. Jeff and I have hunted together, fished together, beached his boat out on Drum Island in Charleston Harbor and gone searching for shark's teeth in the beds of dredge pumped out onto the flats of the island; once, believe it or not, we were stranded in a taxi stuck in a snowstorm in Jordan at the crest of the King's Road, elevation 5000 feet, on our way from Petra to Aqaba and had to be rescued by the Jordanian Army. When my wife Melanie and I lived in France, Jeff and his wife Hart came and visited us, and stayed with us again when we lived in Israel. We went to his mother's funeral in the little Georgia town of Toccoa, where he grew up, one of six children, in a two-room shack. Melanie and I were the only people who weren't family to make the drive from Charleston.

All of which is to say that what Jeff and I talked about on our way home from that quick trip to Fort Campbell wasn't glib, pass-the-time talk. Because we are such close friends, our talk was about what matters to us, and the way we live, and how we parse out and then stitch back together who we are and what we have done and why we do what we do. It was talk borne of a deep and abiding friendship.

And as we drove, the conversation turned to the Heisenberg Uncertainty Principle.

Really.

See, Jeff is the smartest person I know. He recently retired from his practice as one of Charleston's most respected and beloved ear nose and throat doctors. But the whole doctor thing, and the smarts it takes to be not only a doctor but a really good one, is only the tip of the iceberg.

He is a renaissance man. He is a terrific artist – his wildlife drawings have been shown at galleries in Charleston – and he has written and published a novel. He plays the guitar and banjo, both to a fine degree. He is an inventor as well, and one day when you are going in to surgery at a hospital near you, you will be much safer for a device he has created and patented that involves UV light in order to utterly sterilize operating rooms. Though early models of the thing looked like one of those reject droids in the salvage barge in the first *Star Wars* movie, sleeker, cooler models are now in use in a number of hospitals across the country and in Greece and Spain; a German engineering company is running tests on how it will work as an installation into the lighting systems of hospitals yet to be built. The public hospital system in the United Kingdom is also testing it with an eye toward installing them in 1400 units, and three are already in operation in London.

London, by the way, is where he did a fellowship last year at the London School of Tropical Medicine, this because he wants to better serve people living in South Sudan, where he has spent over a year *in toto* serving as a doctor in Dinka villages so remote his clinics have at times been kept safe from gun-toting rebels with a only a ring of thornbushes.

One more thing (and trust me, this figures in): He is at work on a PhD in anthropology, taking courses at the University of South Carolina with people half his age. He's already written his thesis, though he isn't due to finish coursework for another year, and that thesis – on family structures among the Dinka peoples – is under consideration by Oxford University Press. They asked him to send it to them.

But to Heisenberg: Jeff and I were talking about medical missions, and in particular a water missions group with which he is involved, and for which Melanie works. Part of the job of installing these water reclamation systems involves surveying how they affect the third world groups for whom the systems serve; the mission wants to know about life before and after the clean water source has been brought to them – how lives have been changed by that fresh water. Because anthropology is in essence the observation of cultures and societies, we got to talking about the way even an endeavor as benevolent as bringing fresh, drinkable, life-giving water to people who have known only filthy has the possibility of yielding unwanted and even detrimental results: Who in the village runs the water system, and what power does that then give the person? What happens to the communal relationships built and maintained by people used to gathering water from riverbanks or traveling together to a distant well, but who now only stand in line in the middle of the village? What of the possible dependence of the people upon the deliverers of the water-purifying machine, and the need for those benefactors to maintain the system itself against breakdowns?

And, because Jeff is studying anthropology, he began talking about the observer effect, and the way that even surveying people in order to help make certain they are being served as the missions group wishes to serve them is an intrusion, an upsetting of their culture. Simply observing a culture, the Observer Effect maintains, messes with the culture being observed.

We talked then about the way even thinking about what questions to ask – and what answers perhaps the asker wanted to receive – can skew the whole outcome of any such survey. The observer-expectancy effect, or simply observer bias – in which a researcher's perceptions cause him to influence unconsciously the participants of an experiment – can reveal, finally, more about the surveyor than about those being surveyed, not to mention significantly screw up or maybe even destroy the whole experiment. We ask questions we want answers to, and oftentimes we aren't listening to the answers we get because they don't give us what we want to hear, or – even worse – we ask questions that have nothing to do with the real system we are observing.

I know this all sounds abstract, but believe me, we had a fine conversation that applied wholly to the water missions group and its good work, as well as to Jeff's experiences serving the Dinka people and gathering their family stories for his dissertation.

It just so happened that then we started listening to Bill Bryson's book *A Short History of Everything*, and here came through the speakers words about Heisenberg and his Uncertainty Principle, and the news that, in the effort to predict simultaneously an electron's position and its momentum – the key physical quantities of quantum theory – researchers discovered that when you tried to measure one quantity, the other quantity was altered. Trying to measure the velocity of an electron significantly alters its position; measuring its position involves significantly altering its velocity. Therefore, if one is to try to predict an electron's life, one has to get his head around the fact there is no way to predict an electron's life. Our popular models of electrons as stylized little planets zipping in perfect arcs around an atom are in no way representative of the truth of an electron's path: an electron is nowhere; an electron is everywhere. To try and spot it is to change it.

But while I was sitting behind the wheel of my truck and heading down through the Smokies of eastern Tennessee toward the North Carolina border, there lingered in my ears the notion of surveys of third world groups, of benevolent endeavors to bring fresh water to people who had none, of the good and bad of monitoring the ways we serve others. Then into this mix came the fact of the impossibility of trying to see and name and measure and touch upon something as elemental as an electron's path, and suddenly I felt click into place an understanding of something that, for a long long long time, has worked on me – I am trying to avoid using the words *bothered me* here – about teaching creative writing.

That is, I had an epiphany. The same phenomenon happens in a creative writing workshop as happens in the measuring of an electron's speed, and in the installation of a water system, and in the telling of a Dinka family's story to an anthropologist: There is an intrusion upon the real life of the matter at hand.

I know I am not saying anything new here. Anyone who has had a creative writing workshop knows that external observation and input are part and parcel of the endeavor itself.

But what occurred to me, finally, was to ask what effect the workshop has – deeply, truly – on the creation of genuine art.

Don't think I am against workshops. No. I would not be the author of thirteen books if it weren't for a creative writing class I took while I was an RC Cola salesman who'd quit college to pursue a career in soda pop. After a mediocre performance my first two years at Cal State Long Beach I quit, worked for RC, and saw after a year of *that* that sales wasn't what I wanted to do for the rest of my life. So I enrolled in a course at the local community college because I wanted to get back in the groove of having deadlines and assignments before re-enrolling full-time at Cal State that fall. The only night I had free was Tuesday; the only course open on Tuesday nights was Creative Writing. Here I am.

But I also want to say this: Creative writing workshops are about the most unreal model of the writer's life that has ever been concocted. Never in your real life as a writer will a group of people take your writing seriously enough to ask you to write something, and then gather together in one place at one time and discuss it with you. Writing is, finally, a matter of being alone and putting words on paper and hoping they will capture as clearly and deeply as humanly possible the sense of what you are seeing and feeling and discovering as you write those words.

Workshops are in and of themselves observer-based phenomena; although they are definitely *not* the generative moment of art, they are predicated on a belief that observation improves output.

2

I came home from that trip with Jeff and went back to my semester's worth of workshops. But there was something different about the way I looked at my classes, the obtuse angle I suddenly felt between the students and myself, in my head the image of me standing on one side of a canyon, the class on the other, the all of them – well, maybe a few of them – furiously writing their hearts out and then waving their stories at me and shouting across the abyss, *What do you think, Mr. Lott?*

I started wondering what they were all thinking about me, the observer of this thing called a creative writing workshop; then started to wonder what they thought of the other kids in the class, those other observers who would read their work when it was finished; and then thought of the fact some kids in class were friends with each other before they'd ever signed up for the course, while others were absolute strangers to one another. I started wondering about *everything* they were thinking when they wrote these stories.

Of course I had thought of these issues before. Of course I had. But after this particular trip, for the specific purpose of bidding goodbye to my older son, a young man who had been to Iraq and back, who had seen strangers and friends alike killed in the battlefield, and who was now on the eve of entering into the joy and comfort and upheaval and brand-new world a marriage is, and then to have had this conversation about the ineffable nature of art and time and life with my best friend – well, things were different. *I* was different.

I'd had my epiphany. My role as an instructor was somehow different now.

And just as trying to measure an electron in no way measures an electron and a dissertation on Dinka family structures in no way captures the Dinka family structure, I'd seen that workshops do not predict, spot, capture or create art. They cannot. They will not. They won't.

This is because the creation of art is a private affair. It is borne out of solitude, of sitting one's butt flat in a chair at a desk somewhere and putting one word after another after another, and seeing through this laborious rote behavior to another world, a dream, a deep vision of an other-life that becomes more alive than the world in which one is sitting and being alone.

Kafka, in his *Letters to Felice,* wrote of this quality of deep privacy, this integral retreat from humanity in order to find the right words that will allow one to make meaningful art that encounters humanity:

> *Writing means revealing oneself to excess; that utmost of self-revelation and surrender, in which a human being, when involved with others, would feel he was losing himself, and from which, therefore, he will always shrink as long as he is in his right mind . . . even that degree of self-revelation and surrender is not enough for writing. Writing that springs from the surface of existence — when there is no other way and the deeper wells have dried up — is nothing, and collapses the moment a truer emotion makes that surface shake. This is why one can never be alone enough when one writes, why there can never be enough silence around when one writes, why even night is not night enough. This is why there is never enough time at one's disposal, for the roads are long and it is easy to go astray . . .*

And as I insert this quotation into this essay, meant as a piece of grand evidence for my argument that workshops alter the generative moment when art arrives, I am thinking that perhaps at the root of all this claptrap about workshops there might very well be a longing for my own writing life of long ago, the one that seemed genuinely to begin only *after* I had graduated way back in 1984 from UMass Amherst with my MFA.

I must admit to my observer bias of the entire creative writing-industrial complex from which I draw twice-monthly my very manna, this bias the fact I miss the days when, just after graduating with an MFA buttressed by three years of workshops, I was alone, and had now only to write, and to write.

I miss getting up every morning between 4:30 and 5:00 AM and going to the basement of our townhouse apartment in Columbus, Ohio, the city in which I'd gotten a job teaching five sections of remedial English a quarter at Ohio State. Five classes a day, twenty students per class, three quarters a year. Believe it or not, I sorely miss that time, way back when I was embarked on writing the first book, what would one day become *The Man Who Owned Vermont*, though my only tangible literary accomplishments at that point were a handful of published stories; I miss that time when I had to sneak down the stairs and avoid a particularly ornery step that would creak so loudly that our then-toddler and only child Zebulun would wake up, and the entire endeavor to find quiet would crumble around me.

I miss that aloneness, there at a desk in a basement, where the only window was six feet above the floor, a narrow thing that looked out at ground level, and through which I could see stars when I sat down with my mug of instant coffee and piece of toast, before me the life of an RC Cola salesman and the landscape of western Massachusetts, his sales route, and the shambles of his marriage.

Though I get up at 5:00 every day still, and go to my desk to write – I am in the middle of my thirteenth book – I miss that time, because before then, no one – no one – was watching me write. I was the only one on planet

Earth who cared about what was going to happen to this RC salesman; no one else even knew about this guy, and each morning down in that basement were words about him waiting just beyond my reach, words that, if I just listened closely enough to this salesman, would allow me to grab hold of them and put them in the order his actions and thoughts and *heart* showed me was the right way.

Maybe that's where all this comes from: my longing for that time before I'd ever written a single book, that time when it seemed, for a while, night was night enough.

3

So, what did I do with my epiphany about teaching creative writing?

Despite my so-recent realization of the risks of observation, I decided to observe what I was observing: I wrote a questionnaire and took a survey of my students. Not only of my own students, but creative writing students in other classes at the College of Charleston – Carol Ann Davis passed it out to her poetry workshop, and Tony Varallo passed it out to his fiction workshop, and I gave it to my creative nonfiction workshop and to my advanced fiction workshop.

I am not in the habit of taking surveys. I don't like them, because it seems their aim is to find the average, the mean, the lowest common denominator among that being measured, while as a writer of fiction I'm trying to traffic in the anomaly, the out-of-the-norm, even when I'm writing about what generally interests me: normal people (such as they are). And though my bias against surveys runs so deep that when I was hired by the College in 1986 I refused to take the mandatory Myers-Briggs personality assessment, chiefly because I don't want to know what type I am, my bias still didn't stop me from taking *my* survey, because *I* was the one who wanted to get to the heart of my students, and to know what they were thinking of when they were in the private moment of generating a story, essay, or poem. What *I* wanted to know was important stuff.

My questionnaire was a beautifully crafted thing: twelve questions (No. 1: "When I am writing a story, essay, or poem for a workshop, I think about the response the work might receive from the workshop as a whole" and etc.) that sought on a scale of 1 ("Never") to 5 ("I think a great deal about it, and let it influence my work to a large degree") to pierce the mysterious penumbra of the privacy of writing; there was also an introduction simultaneously funny, disarming, smart, and heartfelt (". . . I want honest answers to these questions, and no beret wearing, clove cigarette-smoking, cappuccino sipping *I'm an artist!* heroics: the art of writing insists upon an inner honesty that is coldly ruthless in its assessment of why we do what we do, both in life and in the creation of art. No posing allowed. Tell the truth. . . ."). I even had a section of questions for people who'd been in workshops before the one they were in right now.

It was a beautiful thing. And preposterously stupid, and sadly self-serving.

I received fifty responses, had to throw out two (one because the respondent wrote "zero" in a couple of places instead of using the point scale, the other because the respondent didn't bother to read the questionnaire, and simply wrote down either "yes" or "no" for responses), and found from the forty-eight students left that, well, yes, above all, when they are writing a story, poem, or essay, they are thinking of the teacher's response (3.7 on my 1 to 5 scale). Next in line was the fact they are thinking of the workshop response as a whole (3.0), and coming in third was their thinking of the response the piece would elicit from a specific prior workshop instructor (2.5).

No news here. Students are thinking, in the moment of trying to create art, of the instructor, both present and past, and about those around them in the classroom. Of course the response I would get would be the response I was looking for, though I'd hoped for something different: that our students would be writing only toward the story or poem or essay they were in the midst of creating, trying to let it be itself instead of fashioned with an eye toward the others there in the classroom with them.

But.

A day after the class meeting in which I'd administered the survey, I got an email from a student in one of my workshops. One Lauren Capone, a graduating senior from New Orleans who was planning to take off a year before applying – if she decided she really wanted and needed it – to an MFA program.

It was a long email, one I very much enjoyed for its candor, its clear-eyed freshness of thought. "I found my way into writing late in high school," she wrote. "I wasn't quite sure what I was doing with it; it was the summer after senior year, and I recall simply wanting to get out of the house so I went to coffee shops all day and wrote, or made small sketches in a notebook. I didn't share it with anyone and not because it was private, just because it didn't come to me to do so." She also told of how she sort of backed into workshops: "For a while I took drawing classes, photography, then print-making. But what I found was that the writing was always there. And that of all mediums, it had the potential to contain me, whereas with something like photography, I felt it was too easy and that I could control most everything. So I started considering writing classes."

And because my mission in this whole survey-giving was to try and figure in my sadly academic, 1-to-5-point way what my students were thinking when writing, I quote the following assessment of the worth of a writing workshop, with her permission:

> *The difficulty with workshop is that the written thing is so big, and often treated as a completed piece of writing, when in fact, at least in my case, I am well aware that it needs more work. Additionally I've become less and less concerned with the finished product itself and more in it for the prac-*

tice of writing, and the discoveries therein. I can sometimes benefit from a workshop if it addresses possibilities for further development of the piece; things to try with the writing. As for people feeling confused [about a story], I for one do not frequently think about the fact that someone might be reading the piece. So in class when peers are confused by something, these kinds of things can be helpful [to the author], but judgment calls are difficult. I don't think that we ought to be given these kinds of things that we can grasp onto like a flotation device, I think [a story] needs to be self-perpetuated, because in the world, you don't get these pillows to rest on, you must find them yourself and keep plugging along. With some mental work I've become pretty good with quieting the distracting judgments that can arise in my mind while I am trying to write.

No number my wonderful survey yielded struck me as more on the mark as to the role the workshop ought to have in the creation of art than this remarkable offering, made by a student I was doing my best to observe as being a part of a classroom of students; her email quashed beautifully any further notion I had of asking a pile of stupid questions about what they were thinking about workshops.

So what ought a workshop to be?

When I was a graduate student at UMass, I had the great good fortune to have been selected to be in a creative writing workshop taught by James Baldwin. The class was made up of three students from each of the Five Colleges (UMass, Amherst, Smith, Mt. Holyoke and Hampshire), and we eager students became aware pretty quickly that Mr. Baldwin wasn't much of a workshop instructor. He'd never been in one, much less taught one, and when after turning in our stories and showing up the next week expecting exquisite assessments of the work at hand and how we might make it better, we were sorely disappointed. He had no vocabulary for this endeavor;

he had no spirit for it; he had no means by which to impart to us, from the wellspring of the creation of his own art, the sorts of things we wanted to hear from him: how to improve the dialogue, the setting, the structure, the characters, the plot.

All that crap *we* wanted to talk about.

The problem, we classmates soon realized (among us, though in our chrysalis stages, the novelist Susan Straight and the playwright Suzan-Lori Parks) was with ourselves. We were seeking from him what he could not give; we were expectant electrons in a system waiting to be observed. But he wasn't even looking at us.

This was because he was a *writer*, and not a trafficker in matters of technique.

After a few weeks of this charade called a workshop *we* were putting *him* through, Mr. Baldwin, a soul at once as meek and as dignified as I have ever encountered, turned out to have been giving us something we hadn't been looking for at all, a system we weren't a part of because it was a system we hadn't been interested in: He began to talk to us about art, and literature, and their importance, relevance, and necessity within the life of the writer. He spoke of the need to write, the need to keep writing no matter what, and the redemptive quality a life in art might afford us.

And though we ended up without a clue as to how to make our stories better, we received an extraordinary education nonetheless.

Now *that* was a good workshop.

In 1981 I read *What We Talk About When We Talk About Love*, my first encounter with the work of Raymond Carver and the way he rendered with awesome precision the razor-edge lives of people who might fall apart at any moment, or who might very well hang on to the bitter end. I saw people who mattered to me, and saw that the author's job was to get out of the way of these people and let them speak for themselves, for better and worse, on their way through their own stories.

That was a good workshop, too.

And even the traditional workshop, the sort I've been taking to task with all these words, can be a good workshop. One autumn Tuesday afternoon in Amherst, I walked into the second class meeting of Jay Neugeboren's workshop – Neugeboren a writer whose stories and books were legend among us. I'd handed in my story the week before, and sat down to see my work examined in the most traditional of ways, each student there weighing in one way and another, Jay patiently leading and prodding, then stepping up at the end with his own two cents.

He liked it. He suggested this and that, things here and there. He suggested ways to make it a better story in the traditional ways a workshop teacher can suggest. More importantly, the careful and generous and even-handed way in which he let us express our views and then expressed his own made me a better writer, one who could sit alone and write stories those early mornings and then feel confident that the response they might receive in class would be just, and genuine, and true. His workshop was a gift to me, and led to my choosing him to be the mentor of my work while at UMass.

The story I turned in? A little thing – seven pages – about a rocky moment within a young marriage. "I Owned Vermont" would be its eventual title.

Hebrews 12:12 is a verse that comes at the end of a passage in which Paul exhorts his readers to remember everyone of faith – from Abel to Abraham to Moses to Rahab to the nameless men and women martyred through the ages – and their perseverance in that faith: "Therefore we also, since we are surrounded by so great a cloud of witnesses, let us lay aside every weight, and the sin which so easily ensnares us, and let us run the race that is set before us."

The witnesses – that great cloud – aren't, as is often thought, some sort of swirling mass of spirit entities watching what we are doing as we do it, so that you better watch out, you better not cry, you better not pout, Paul's telling you why. No. Rather, what is meant by the word *witness* here is the quality of the lives lived before ours; the measure of faith, and life in that faith, that each brought to his or her relationship to our creator God; it is the example, if I may, of the artistry by which each lived his or her life in service to that God.

I think, finally, that the best workshop we can have might very well be with our own cloud of witnesses, people who went before us *and* people who are still among us, whose lives in art – that is, whose giving of fresh and enlivening water through their words – most affect us.

My witnesses include Baldwin, and Carver, and Neugeboren. But chief among them has to be Flannery O'Connor, who wrote,

> One thing that is always with the writer – no matter how long he has written or how good he is – is the continuing process of learning how to write. As soon as the writer "learns to write," as soon as he knows what he is going to find, and discovers a way to say what he knew all along, or worse still, a way to say nothing, he is finished. If a writer is any good, what he makes will have its source in a realm much larger than that which his conscious mind can encompass and will always be a greater surprise to him that it can ever be to his reader.

Yet another key witness for me is John Steinbeck, who wrote on the eighteenth day of the journal he kept while writing *The Grapes of Wrath* – he completed the book in 100 days – "If only I could do this book properly it would be one of the really fine books and a truly American book. But I am assailed with my own ignorance and inability. I'll just have to work from a background of these." I come in close contact with my own ignorance and inability every time I touch the keyboard, and to know Steinbeck wrote that book in full embrace of his own gives me the courage I need to move forward, in spite of me.

Perhaps the newest member of this workshop of witnesses is Lauren Capone, who reminds me that it takes mental work to quiet the distracting judgments that arise when I am trying to write.

This is because writing occurs within an immeasurable moment, in the privacy of the way synapses fire within the brain, layering one snap onto another until an image occurs, begins to breathe, then stands up and walks its way through nerves into muscles into the fingertips and onto the hard plastic of a keyboard, or through the smallest kiss of a pen on paper.

This moment is incredibly brittle, ready to break at the smallest creak of a stairway step or gulp of cold coffee. To call this act of synapse to finger-tips *writing* is to describe it in the most rudimentary way, revealing to no real extent what the engaged imagination is in the act of doing: creating a new world.

What I think I may be understanding, now that the whole of this moment of measuring the immeasurable is over, now that my clever numbers have been recorded and tossed away, is that the business I ought to be about in the workshops I teach is to be not only the teacher but also a writer, there at my desk at 5:00 each morning with my coffee and the next new world I am imagining. As the observer observing, I must first and foremost be the best witness I can be.

As I write this, Zeb is now married. Jeff Deal is in Honduras, working to provide potable water to villagers high in the mountains. A new flareup of tribal killings has occurred in Wernyol in South Sudan, and the weather this moment on the King's Road to Aqaba is a warm 88 degrees.

That is, the electron-world is busy spinning, being itself.

And I am here, however preposterously stupid or sadly self-serving, writing this; trying to find with each word when night is night enough; trying to write, and to be writing.

FLAKES

Fred Chappell

Anticipation of Snow

the street is holding its breath
the light withholding its breadth

Night Snow

she has dropped her cotton bathrobe
and hides naked in the sunrise

Snow Dawn

its light fills the windows
with more revelation
than ever was promised

Daybreak Snowfield

no thought so bold
it dare make its mark here

Begin Again

the snow finds that everything that was lost
is not lost

Peace-at-Last Snowfield

a quarrel of sharp
symmetrical geometries
has been harmoniously resolved.

The Snowfield

a million uniquenesses produce
one silent anonymity

Aurora

snow-lawn, thin mist, sunrise:
a white house blushes

After the Snowfall

first in my neighborhood to slip outside
I feel I am breaking and entering

Inspiration

this deep uncustomary snowfall
has made the world so quiet
I hear poems being scribbled
all over town

Rapt

the cat is observing the snowfall

black
cat

watches

snow

fall

Bright Combat

the snow's invincible shining
has driven the moon to shelter in a cloud

Snow Patches

what awkward wounds earth must have sustained
to be so raggedly bandaged

Snow Melt

the big puffy chrysalis at curbside
is hatching a moth-blue Volkswagen

ANTHONY S. ABBOTT is the author of two novels and five books of poetry, the latest of which, *New and Selected Poems, 1989-2009*, was published in 2009. His novel, *Leaving Maggie Hope*, won the Novello Award in 2003. He is Professor Emeritus of English at Davidson College and President of the NC Poetry Society.

JULIA ALVAREZ was raised in the Dominican Republic and emigrated to the United States in 1960. She is the author of the critically acclaimed novels, *How The Garcia Girls Lost Their Accents* and *In The Time of the Butterflies* (a National Book Critics Circle Award finalist). She lives in Middlebury, Vermont, with her husband and teaches writing classes at Middlebury College.

 NATHALIE F. ANDERSON has authored three books: *Following Fred Astaire* (winner of the 1998 Washington Prize from The Word Works), *Crawlers* (winner of the 2005 McGovern Prize from Ashland Poetry Press) and *Quiver*. She has authored libretti for three operas – *The Black Swan*, *Sukey in the Dark*, and *A Scandal in Bohemia* – in collaboration with composer Thomas Whitman and Philadelphia's Orchestra. Anderson teaches at Swarthmore College, where she is a Professor in the Department of English Literature and directs the Program in Creative Writing.

JOSEPH BATHANTI is the author of six books of poetry: *Communion Partners; Anson County; The Feast of All Saints; This Metal*, nominated for The National Book Award, and winner of the 1997 Oscar Arnold Young Award; *Land of Amnesia*, and *Restoring Sacred Art*, winner of 2010 Roanoke Chowan Award, given annually by the NC Literary and Historical Association. His novels are *East Liberty*, winner of the Carolina Novel Award; and *Coventry*, winner of the Novello Literary Award. *They Changed the State: The Legacy of North Carolina's Visiting Artists, 1971-1995* is his book of nonfiction. His collection of short stories, *The High Heart*, won the 2007 Spokane Prize. Bathanti teaches at Appalachian State University.

 KATHRYN STRIPLING BYER's first book of poetry won the Associated Writing Programs Award Series in 1986. Her subsequent collections include: *Wildwood Flower* (the 2002 Lamont Selection of the Academy of American Poets), *Black Shawl*, *Catching Light*, and *Coming to Rest*, which received the Hanes Award from the Fellowship of Southern Writers. She served as North Carolina's first woman Poet Laureate from 2005 to 2010.

In 2004 FRED CHAPPELL retired after 40 years in the English Department of the University of North Carolina Greensboro. During this period, he published 26 books of poetry, fiction, and critical commentary. Various awards have been conferred upon him, most recently (2010) the John Tyler Caldwell Award. For five years he served as North Carolina's Poet Laureate and in that capacity visited some 250 schools, colleges, universities, retirement homes, churches, and other venues. His latest book of poetry is *Shadow Box*, latest fiction, *Ancestors and Others: New and Selected Stories*. Fred and his wife Susan live in Greensboro, tending cats, plants, and (mostly) their own business.

RICHARD CHESS is the author of three books of poetry *Tekiah, Chair in the Desert*, and *Third Temple*. He directs The Center for Jewish Studies at UNC-Asheville as well as UNC- Asheville's Creative Writing Program.

BILLY COLLINS served as Poet Laureate of the United States from 2001 to 2003. During that time he created the program, Poetry 180, giving high school students a poem a day to read for the 180 days of their school year. He is the recipient of Fellowships from the National Endowment from the Arts and the Guggenheim Foundation. In 1994 he was named poet of the year by *Poetry Magazine*. He is a Distinguished Professor at Lehman College of the City of New York.

ABIGAIL DEWITT is the author of two novels, *Lili* and *Dogs*. Currently at work on a collection, *The Sex Appeal of the French & Other Stories*, she lives in the mountains of NC with her husband and daughter. In 2010, she was the Visiting Writer-in-Residence at Lenoir-Rhyne University.

NIKKI GIOVANNI writes children's literature, essays and adult poetry. She is the winner of seven NAACP Image Awards and her book *Rosa* was a Caldecott Honors winner.

MITCHELL GOLD is the co-founder of Mitchell Gold + Bob Williams. He is also the founder of Faith in America, a non-profit organization dedicated to educating people about religion-based bigotry. Gold is the editor of *CRISIS: 40 Stories Revealing the Personal, Social and Religious Trauma of Growing up Gay in America.* and the co-author, along with Bob Williams, of *Let's Get Comfortable* and *The Comfortable Home*.

R.S. GWYNN has taught at Lamar University since 1976. He is the author of *No Word of Farewell: Selected Poems 1970-2000* and is the editor of the Penguin Pocket Anthology series.

SEAMUS HEANEY was born in Northern Ireland in 1939, but has lived in the Republic of Ireland since 1972. He has taught at Queen's University, Belfast, and from 1982-1996 spent one term a year at Harvard. In 1995 Heaney was awarded the Nobel Prize for Literature. He has published twelve books of poems, three books of critical essays and several translations.

Born and raised in Red Wing, Minnesota, ROBERT HEDIN is the author, translator, and editor of 22 books of poetry and prose. Honors for his work include three National Endowment for the Arts Fellowships. He has taught at the University of Alaska, St. Olaf College, and Wake Forest University. He is co-founder and current director of the Anderson Center in Red Wing, and co-edits Great River Review.

JOSEPHINE HUMPHREYS is the author of four novels, the most recent of which is *Nowhere Else on Earth*. Her work has won a Guggenheim Fellowship, the Southern Book Award, and an award in literature from the American Academy of Arts and Letters. She is a member of the Fellowship of Southern Writers and lives on Sullivan's Island near Charleston, S.C.

ROBERT INMAN is the author of four novels: *Home Fires Burning, Old Dogs and Children, Dairy Queen Days*, and *Captain Saturday*; and a non-fiction work, *Coming Home: Life, Love and All Things Southern*. His playwriting credits include *Crossroads, The Christmas Bus, Dairy Queen Days, Welcome to Mitford, A High Country Christmas Carol, The Christmas Bus: The Musical*, and *The Drama Club*. He has written screenplays for six motion pictures for television, two of which have been "Hallmark Hall of Fame" presentations. Inman is an Alabama native and a North Carolina resident since 1970.

BRET LOTT is the bestselling author of twelve books, including the novels *Jewel*, an Oprah Book Club pick, and *Ancient Highway*. He has served as a Fulbright Senior American Scholar and writer-in-residence at Bar-Ilan University in Tel Aviv, Israel; has spoken on Flannery O'Connor at The White House; and is a member of the National Council on the Arts. He teaches at The College of Charleston, and lives with his wife, Melanie, in Hanahan, South Carolina.

JOAN MCBREEN is from Sligo, Ireland. She divides her time between Tuam and Renvyle, County Galway. Her four poetry collections include *Winter in the Eye – New and Selected Poems* and *Heather Island.* She has compiled and edited two anthologies, *The White Page – An Bhileog Bhan-Twentieth-Century Irish Women Poets* and *The Watchful Heart – A New Generation of Irish Poets, Poems and Essays.* Her papers are archived in the Special Collections Department (Contemporary Irish Literature) at the Robert W. Woodruff Library, Emory University, Atlanta, Georgia.

JILL MCCORKLE is a professor in the MFA in Creative Writing program at NC State. She has taught at UNC-Chapel Hill, Tufts University and Brandeis, where she was the Fannie Hurst Visiting Writer. She was a Briggs-Copeland Lecturer in Creative Writing at Harvard. A member of the Fellowship of Southern Writers, McCorkle has the distinction of having published her first two novels on the same day in 1984. Since then, she has published three other novels and four collections of short stories.

FRANK MCCOURT was born in Brooklyn, NY, in 1930 and grew up in Ireland, the setting for his Pulitzer Prize winning biography, *Angela's Ashes.* As a young man he returned to America, where he ended up teaching in the New York City Public School System for 27 years, the subject of his memoir, *Teacher Man.*

SHARON OLDS is the author of nine books of poetry, including *The Dead and the Living,* winner of the National Book Critics Circle Award, *The Unswept Room,* finalist for the National Book Award and the National Book Critics Circle, and *One Secret Thing,* a finalist for the Forward Prize. She is a Chancellor of the Academy of American Poets and teaches graduate poetry workshops at New York University.

MARK POWELL is the author of the novels *Prodigals* and *Blood Kin,* the latter of which won the Peter Taylor Prize for the Novel, and has received fellowships from National Endowment for the Arts and the Breadloaf Writers' Conference. He teaches at Stetson University in Florida.

REYNOLDS PRICE (1933-2011) lived virtually his whole life in his native North Carolina, except for a period of three years as a Rhodes Scholar at Merton College, Oxford. He taught at his Alma Mater, Duke University, where he spent one semester each year in the classroom and the other writing. Novelist, essayist, poet, playwright, scholar—he is perhaps best remembered for his first novel, *A Long and Happy Life* (1962) and for his stirring memoir of his battle with cancer, *A Whole New Life (1994).*

ANNA QUINDLEN is best known as a journalist and columnist. Her columns for the *New York Times* won the Pulitzer Prize for Commentary in 1992. In 1995 she left the Times to become a full-time novelist. From 1999 to 2009 she wrote a regular column for *Newsweek* magazine. She and her husband, Gerald Krovatin, live in New York City and have three children.

RON RASH is the author of twelve books, the most recent *Burning Bright*. He teaches at Western Carolina University in North Carolina.

DORI SANDERS grew up near York, South Carolina. She does most of her writing in the winter months and reserves her time during the peach growing season for work on the family farm and at Sanders' Farm Stand. She is the author of two best-selling novels, *Clover* and *Her Own Place*. In addition, she is the author of *Dori Sanders' Country Cooking* and *Promise Land: A Farmer Remembers*.

DONALD SECREAST teaches composition, fiction writing, and literature at Radford University. Presently, he's working on a book entitled *Catching the Narrative Wave: Using Microsoft Excel to Teach Close Reading*. He has demonstrated this technique at CEA conferences in Virginia and Puerto Rico. His most recent publication is an essay about how to introduce students to analytical topic sentences: "Physics for English Majors: How to Construct a Death Ray for Generalities," which appeared in the Fall 2009/Winter 2010 issue of *The Virginia English Bulletin*.

LEE SMITH is the author of 15 works of fiction including *Oral History, Fair and Tender Ladies*, and her recent *On Agate Hill*. Her novel *The Last Girls* was a 2002 *New York Times* bestseller as well as winner of the Southern Book Critics Circle Award. A retired professor of English at North Carolina State University, she has received many awards including the North Carolina Award for Literature; and an Academy Award in Fiction from the American Academy of Arts and Letters. Her latest collection of new and selected stories, *Mrs. Darcy and the Blue-Eyed Stranger*, was published in March 2010.

CATHY SMITH BOWERS' poems have appeared in publications including *The Atlantic Monthly, The Georgia Review,* and *Poetry*. She is the author of four books, including *The Love that Ended Yesterday in Texas* (inaugural winner of the Texas Tech University Press First Book Competition, 1992). She teaches in the Queens' MFA in Creative Writing Program in Charlotte, NC, and at Wofford College. She was appointed North Carolina's Poet Laureate in 2010 and lives in Tryon, NC.

ELEANORA E. TATE is the author of eleven books for children, including *Celeste's Harlem Renaissance*, a 2008 IRA Teachers' Choice Award winner; and *Just an Overnight Guest* (made into an award-winning film). In 1990 she was honored by the South Carolina House and Senate for her literary achievements and community activism. A 1999 Zora Neal Hurston Award recipient, she's had numerous pieces published in magazines and scholarly journals. She's on the faculty of Hamline University's low-residency Masters program and is an instructor with the Institute of Children's Literature.

RHETT ISEMAN TRULL's first book, *The Real Warnings*, received the 2008 Anhinga Prize for Poetry, 2010 Devil's Kitchen Reading Award, 2010 Brockman-Campbell Book Award, and 2010 Oscar Arnold Young Award. Her work has appeared in *The American Poetry Review*, *Best New Poets 2008*, *Prairie Schooner*, *The Southern Review*, and other publications. She and her husband Jeff Trull publish *Cave Wall* in Greensboro, North Carolina.

 JOHN UPDIKE, a native of Pennsylvania, was the foremost American novelist of the second half of the twentieth century, most famous for his "Rabbit" tetralogy. *Rabbit is Rich (1981)* and *Rabbit at Rest (1991)*, the third and fourth novels in the series, both received Pulitzer Prizes in fiction, a rare achievement. His early novel, *The Centaur* (1963) won the National Book Award. The prolific Updike also wrote poetry, short stories, essays on a wide variety of subjects and art criticism.

MICHAEL WATERS' recent books include *Gospel Night*, *Selected Poems*, and *Darling Vulgarity*, a finalist for the *Los Angeles Times* Book Prize. His awards include four Pushcart Prizes and fellowships from the NEA and Fulbright Foundation. He teaches at Monmouth University and in the Drew University MFA Program in Poetry and Poetry in Translation, and lives in Ocean, NJ.

1988

Paul Muldoon

1989–1990

Robert Hedin
Nathalie Anderson
Michael Waters
Jennifer Jordan

1990–1991

Derek Mahon
Helen Vendler
Eamon Grennan
David Bottoms
Olga Broumas
Charles Simic
Donald Seacrest
Linda Lightsey Rice
Eiléan Ní Chuilleanáin
John Skoyles
Linda Brown Bragg
Betty Adcock
Richard Murphy

1991–1992

Michael Yeats
Declan Kiberd
Dori Sanders
Sarah Gilbert
Nuala Ní Dhomhnaill
Nola Richardson
Betty Adcock
Seamus Heaney

1992–1993

Lee Smith
Gerald Barrax
Chuck Sullivan
Fiona Cheong
Fred Chappell
Linda Lightsey Rice
John Montague

1993–1994

Reynolds Price
James Applewhite
Deborah Pope
Susan Ludvigson
Linda Lightsey Rice
Donald Davis

1994–1995

Ellen Gilchrist
Scott Owens
Bret Lott
Kate Daniels
Dannye Romine Powell
Ciaran Carson
R. S. Gwynn
Terry Gifford
Billy Collins

1995–1996

Steven Yount
Kathryn Stripling Byer
Julie Kate Howard
Betty Adcock
Kaye Gibbons

Mark & Gail
Mathabane
Todd McEwen
Marie Heaney
Ruthanne Lum
McCunn

1996–1997

Michael Longley
Clyde Edgerton
Wilma Dykeman
Eleanora E. Tate
Terry Gifford
Ron Whitehead
Peter Fallon
James Welch
Nigel Jenkins
Menna Elfyn
Iwan Llwyd

1997–1998

Jill McCorkle
Billy Collins
Paul Muldoon
Dori Sanders
Robert Inman
Saleem Peeradina
Ernest J. Gaines
J. California Cooper
Todd McEwen

1998–1999

Lee Smith
Lee Eric Shackleford
Lewis Nordan

E. Ethelbert Miller
Jan Karon
Jorge Velasco Mackenzie
Jade Ngoc Quang
Huynh
Shelby Foote
John Shelton Reed
Kathryn Stripling Byer

1999–2000

Yusef Komunyakaa
Linda Beatrice Brown
Donald Hall
Adrian Rice
Nathalie Anderson
Jill Jones
Robert Morgan
Sue Ellen Bridgers
Luis Rodriguez
Orson Scott Card
Joseph Bathanti
Leslie Marmon Silko
Connie Briscoe

2000–2001

Carolyn Kizer
Ernest Suarez
Pat Conroy
Eavan Boland
Joe Connelly
Afaa M. Weaver
Ron Rash
Michael Strickland
Lucinda Roy
Benjamin Alire Sáenz

2001–2002

Richard Chess
Robert Conley
Nicolae Dabija
Bret Lott
Josephine Humphreys
John Stone, MD
Nikki Giovanni
R. T. Smith
Kyle Gann
Leroy Quintana

2002–2003

Coleman Barks
Seamus Heaney
Bill Bryson
Marilyn Nelson
Amiri Baraka (LeRoi Jones)
Mary Hood
Saleem Peeradina

2003–2004

Billy Collins
Joan McBreen
Kathy Reichs
Richard Ford
Michael Knight
Karen Joy Fowler
Martín Espanda

2004–2005

Ron Whitehead
Anne Fadiman

Jonathan Lethem
Thomas Lynch
Sharon Olds
Bob Inman
Alice Walker
Adrian Rice
Dale Bailey

2005–2006

l thi diem thúy
Frank Deford
Joyce Carol Oates
Kelly Link
Naomi Shihab Nye
Tim O'Brien

2006–2007

James Bradley
John Updike
Anthony S. Abbott
Nikkey Finney
Gary Snyder
James McBride **
Christopher Paul Curtis*

2007–2008

Thomas Rain Crowe
Duchess of Abercorn
Walter Isaacson
Frank McCourt
Tracy Kidder
Mark Powell
Jane Smiley
Jon Scieszka*

2008–2009

Galway Kinnell
Anna Quindlen
Jonathan Kozol
Terry McMillan
Julie Fay
Geraldine Brooks**
Bruce Lansky*

SPIRIT OF BLACK
MOUNTAIN COLLEGE

Ted Pope
Lee Ann Brown
Lisa Jarnot
Thomas Meyer
Jeff Davis
Michael Rumaker
Thomas Rain Crowe

2009–2010

Richard Rodriguez
Marisha Pessl
Tess Gallagher
Paula Meehan
Jeannette Walls
Paula Vogel
Mitchell Gold
Abigail DeWitt
Julia Alvarez*

2010–2011

John Feinstein
Joan McBreen
Cathy Smith Bowers
Rhett Iseman Trull

A. J. Jacobs
Luis Alberto Urrea
John Granger
W. S. Merwin
Amina McIntyre
Kevin Young
David Baldacci
Deborah Wiles*

* The Little Read
** The Big Read

259